JOURNEY THROUGH THE NEW TESTAMENT

JOURNEY THROUGH THE NEW TESTAMENT

STAN DEKOVEN

Vision Publishing · Ramona, California

JOURNEY THROUGH THE NEW TESTAMENT

FOR INFORMATION ON ORDERING PLEASE CONTACT:

VISION PUBLISHING
1520 Main Street, C
RAMONA, CA 92065
760-789-4700
WWW.VISION.EDU

PRINTED IN THE UNITED STATES OF AMERICA

TABLE OF CONTENTS

FOREWORD

There is no greater book than the Holy Bible. To the Christian believer, the words of Christ and the purposes of His church found in the New Testament are vital to life and growth. There is no greater calling than the call to the ministry of that Word. Contained within the pages of the Bible is a story of such magnitude that it is beyond human capacity to fully comprehend. In spite of that fact, we must, as the people of God, do all we can to understand the meaning, message, and purpose of God's Holy Book.

It has been said that the most difficult part of doing anything is to begin. Whether reading a book, starting a diet, or pursuing a new career, motivating oneself to begin the journey is the key to ultimate success. The mere fact that you have opened this book indicates a desire to study to show yourself approved. You are to be commended for taking the first step.

This book on New Testament survey has been written with three audiences in mind. The first target "audience" is the teacher of the Word of God who is searching for a concise guide to this awesome topic. The second group is the individual Bible college student who needs a thorough overview of God's Word, given in a book-by-book fashion, to lay some foundation for further biblical study. The final group is the adult learner (age 14 years and above) who wants a quick grasp of the Bible as God's special revelation to mankind.

As you begin the New Testament journey, keep an open heart so that the Holy Spirit, who originally inspired the revelation of Scripture, will bring understanding and revelation to you. God's precious Word is truly a lamp unto your feet, and a light into your path. Hide the Word in your heart (Psalm 119:105).

INTRODUCTION

(This introduction is similar to that found in *Journey Through the Old Testament*, and is repeated here for those who have not taken that course.)

The New Testament can be surveyed in several different ways:
1. By studying the lives of the main Bible characters
2. By studying themes such as "the blood," "the covenants," etc.
3. By working out the chronological order of the events
4. By determining what was happening in the rest of the world to give perspective
5. By studying each book in order
6. By studying the history and culture of the peoples

Other important items of note and specific helps include:
1. Who were the authors?
   - Kings and princes, poets, philosophers, prophets, statesmen, unschooled fisher-men, a tax gatherer, etc.

2. What are the principle elements?
   - Principle places
   - Principle facts
   - Principle periods

3. The Bible is one story, one history, His story, the story of Jesus Christ.
   - All through the ages we find the promise of a Savior (Matthew 20:28; Luke 19:10).

4. The Bible can be read in approximately 80 hours. Please do not dip in here or there, but instead read systematically.

5. No Scripture should be privately interpreted, but Scripture is to interpret Scripture (Peter 1:20). However, the Holy Spirit has promised to lead us into all truth (John 16:13).

6. The Old Testament is an account of a nation. The New Testament is an account of a Man (the Son of man). The nation was founded and nurtured by God to be a vehicle to bring the Man into the world (Genesis 12:1-3).

7. God became a man so that we might know what to think of when we think of God (John 1:14, 14:9).
   - His appearance on the earth is the central event of all history. The Old Testament sets the stage. The New Testament describes it.
   - He is not a historical character - dead and gone, but a living Person - the most vital force in the world today.

8. The Word (Adapted from *What the Bible is All About* by Henrietta C. Mears.)
   - It is God-given (2 Timothy 3:10-17).
   - It should be treasured (Deuteronomy 11:1-9; Joshua 1:8-9).
   - It should be kept (Psalm 119:9-18).
   - It is a lamp (Psalm 119:105-117).
   - It is food (Isaiah 55:1-5; Matthew 4:4).
   - It has been and is being fulfilled (Luke 24:36-45).
   - It is complete (Revelation 22:8-21).

Therefore, we must systematically study God's Word. Let us first look at the Word of God as it is organized, to give us a clearer understanding.

The Old Testament - Foundation and History of a People
The Old Testament consists of 39 books. In these books we find the history of God's dealings with a people and the foundation for the revelation to come in the New Testament. Many scholars have stated that there is no need for the study of the Old Testament since the birth of Christ. They feel that only the Gospels and the Book of Revelation matter,

because in their way of reasoning, the old is "passed away." This concept is, of course, absurd. All of God's Word is precious and significant. Jesus and the Apostles taught from the Old Testament. Our foundation of faith is presented there. Further, we are told in Hebrews that the Old Testament carries the types of things to come. We need to understand the Old Testament to clearly understand the New Testament.

Books of the Old Testament

History 17	Experience 5	Prophecy 17
Basic Law 5 Pre-Exile 9 Post-Exile 3	Inner Life 5	Basic Prophecy 5 Pre-Exile 9 Post-Exile 3
Moses Canaan Exiles	Heart	5 Major 12 Minor

We can begin to reduce the 39 books of the Old Testament into three major divisions: History, Experience, and Prophecy. Under these divisions we have sections of emphasis which will be further broken down throughout the text. Under History there are 17 books in all. We have sections of Basic Law, consisting of five books (Genesis, Exodus, Leviticus, Numbers and Deuteronomy); the nine pre-exile books (Joshua, Judges, Ruth, 1 and 2 Samuel, 1 and 2 Kings, 1 and 2 Chronicles); and the three post-exile books (Ezra, Nehemiah, and Esther).

The Experience books reveal the inner life of the heart, teaching us about God's wisdom and man's folly, the place and power of praise and worship of our Almighty God, and the futility of self-service ventures. These books also teach how to face suffering. These books include Job, Psalms, Proverbs, Ecclesiastes, and Song of Solomon.

Finally, we see the 17 books of Prophecy, of which five (Isaiah, Jeremiah, Lamentations, Ezekiel, and Daniel) are considered major, and twelve (Hosea, Joel, Amos, Obadiah, Jonah, Micah, Nahum, Habakkuk, Zephaniah, Haggai, Zechariah, and Malachi) are referred to as minor prophets.

When studying the Old Testament (or Old Covenant as it is also known), it is important to remember that the books cannot be separated from the people. The Old Testament reveals to us a picture of a people in

11

relationship with their God. From the beginning, God Almighty has been a covenant making and keeping God. He has desired a relationship with a people, the Hebrew people, and the Old Testament chronicles the story of His marvelous dealings with this most remarkable and resilient culture.

While reading the Old Testament, it is important to recognize the great love of God for the Hebrews, as well as His absolute demand for holiness. When the people of God obeyed the commands and kept the covenant of God, prosperity, blessings, health, and protection were afforded them. When rebellion entered in, along with the subsequent sins of idolatry, fornication, etc., a decline and eventual punishment ensued. However, lest we sense that God is cruel, we should notice the marvelous promises and fulfillments of promises by God to restore His people.

Finally, the Old Testament was, as is well put by the writer of the Book of Hebrews, a type and shadow of things to come. Through our study of the Old Testament, we gain an understanding of God's dealings in our lives as we apply the types and shadows to our understanding.

Those who would say that the Old Testament is no longer necessary for godly instruction miss out on the revelation it contains.

The New Testament - The Revelation of Christ: Redemption Fulfilled
The New Testament consists of 27 individual books or letters. In these books can be found the revelation of God's love for mankind fulfilled in Christ's death and resurrection. Further, we find the history of Jesus, the Apostles, and the early church, as well as the various letters (epistles) of instruction and doctrine necessary for Christian living. In each page, one senses the pulsing of God's love and compassion for all mankind.

New Testament History

Historical Foundations	Pastoral Experience	Personal Experience	Doctrine
Matthew	Romans	Titus	Hebrews
Mark	1 & 2 Corinthians	1 & 2 Timothy	James
Luke	Galatians	Philemon	1 & 2 Peter
John	Ephesians		1, 2, 3 John
Acts	Philippians		Jude
	Colossians		Revelation
	1 & 2 Thessalonians		

As with the Old Testament, it is helpful to reduce the 27 books of the New Testament into categories. For our study, we will divide the New Testament into three divisions.

The first division has to do with the historic foundations of the church and includes five books (Matthew, Mark, Luke, John, and Acts). For the second and third divisions we see a combination of experience and doctrine broken down further into nine Christian church letters (Romans, 1 and 2 Corinthians, Galatians, Ephesians, Philippians, Colossians, 1 and 2 Thessalonians); four pastoral and personal letters (Titus, 1 and 2 Timothy, and Philemon); and nine doctrinal epistles (Hebrews, James, 1 and 2 Peter, 1, 2, and 3 John, Jude, and Revelation). These are arbitrary divisions intended to help in the study of the New Testament.

As with the Old Testament, systematic study of God's Word is essential. The student should begin his or her study by reading the Word of God with the perspectives outlined in this text. However, it must be recognized that the Holy Spirit is sovereign and can and will guide into all truth. The student must keep his or her heart open to the Holy Spirit as the study of God's Word begins.

Eras, Key Figures, and Locations
Throughout this book the student will find mention of eras (time frame), locations (where the book was written, and where events took place), and key figures for that particular book. I have summarized each of them

by Old and New Testament (taken from *30 Days to Understanding the Bible*, by Max E. Anders).

Old Testament

Era	Key Figure	Location
1. Creation	Adam	Eden
2. Patriarch	Abraham	Canaan
3. Exodus	Moses	Egypt
4. Conquest	Joshua	Canaan
5. Judges	Samson/Gideon	Canaan
6. Kingdom	David	Israel
7. Exile	Daniel	Babylonia
8. Return	Ezra/Nehemiah	Jerusalem
9. Silence	Pharisees	Jerusalem

New Testament

Era	Key Figure	Location
1. Gospels	Jesus	Palestine
2. Church	Peter	Jerusalem
3. Missions	Paul	Roman Empire

PART 1
INTRODUCTION TO THE BIBLE

ONE

INTRODUCING THE BIBLE

Objectives
Upon completion of this chapter you will be able to:
- Write the key verses from memory
- Define the word *Bible*
- Define the word *Scripture*
- Explain the origin of the Bible
- Identify the major purposes of the Bible
- Identify the Old and New Testaments as the two major divisions of the Bible
- Name the four divisions of the Old Testament books
- Name the four divisions of the New Testament books
- Explain what is meant by "the unity and diversity" of the Bible
- Identify the person upon whom the revelation of both testaments center

Key Verses
All Scripture is inspired by God and profitable for teaching, for reproof, for correction, for training in righteousness; so that the man of God may be adequate, equipped for every good work (2 Timothy 3:16-17).

Introduction

This chapter introduces the Bible, which is the written Word of the one true God. The word *Bible* means "the books." The Bible is one volume which consists of 66 separate books.

The word *Scripture* is also used to refer to God's Word. This word comes from a Latin word which means "writing." When the word *scripture* is used with a capital "S," it means the sacred writings of the one true God. The word *Bible* is not used in the Bible. It is a word selected by men as a title for all of God's Words.

Origin of the Bible

The Bible is the written Word of God. He inspired the words in the Bible and used approximately forty different men to write down His words. These men wrote God's words over a period of 1,500 years. The perfect agreement of these writers is one proof that they were all guided by a single author. That author was God.

Some of the writers wrote down exactly what God said: *"Take a scroll and write on it all the words which I have spoken to you concerning Israel"* (Jeremiah 36:2).

Other writers wrote what they experienced or what God revealed concerning the future: *"Therefore write the things which you have seen, and the things which are, and the things which will take place after these things"* (Revelation 1:19).

All of the writers wrote, under God's inspiration, the words of His message for us.

The Purpose of the Bible

The Bible itself records its main purpose: *"All Scripture is inspired by God and profitable for teaching, for reproof, for correction, for training in righteousness; so that the man of God may be adequate, equipped for every good work"* (2 Timothy 3:16-17).

The Scriptures are to be used to teach doctrine, to reprove and correct from evil, and to teach about righteousness. They will help you live right and equip you to work for God.

18

Major Divisions

The Bible is divided into two major sections called the Old Testament and the New Testament. The word *testament* means "covenant." A covenant is an agreement. The Old Testament records God's original covenant or agreement with man. The New Testament records the new covenant made by God through His Son, Jesus Christ.

What was the subject of these two agreements? They both concerned restoring sinful man to right relationship with God. God made a law that only through the shedding of blood could sin be forgiven: *"Without shedding of blood there is no forgiveness"* (Hebrews 9:22).

Under God's agreement in the Old Testament, blood sacrifices of animals were made by man to obtain forgiveness for sin. This sacrificing of animals was a symbol of the blood sacrifice Jesus Christ would provide under the new agreement with God. The old covenant was in effect until God sent Jesus to establish a new relationship with man.

Through the birth, life, death, and resurrection of Jesus, a final sacrifice for sin was made:

But when Christ appeared as a high priest of the good things to come, He entered through the greater and more perfect tabernacle, not made with hands, that is to say, not of this creation; and not through the blood of goats and calves, but through His own blood, He entered the holy place once for all, having obtained eternal redemption. For if the blood of goats and bulls and the ashes of a heifer sprinkling those who have been defiled sanctify for the cleansing of the flesh, how much more will the blood of Christ, who through the eternal Spirit offered Himself without blemish to God, cleanse your conscience from dead works to serve the living God? For this reason He is the mediator of a new covenant, so that, since a death has taken place for the redemption of the transgressions that were committed under the first covenant, those who have been called may receive the promise of the eternal inheritance (Hebrews 9:11-15).

Both testaments are the Word of God, and we must study both in order to understand God's message. The terms *old* and *new* testaments are

19

used to distinguish between God's agreement with man before and after the death of Jesus Christ. We do not disregard the Old Testament simply because it is called "old."

Further Divisions
The Bible is further divided into 66 books. The Old Testament has 39 books. The New Testament contains 27 books. Each book is divided into chapters and verses. Although the content of each book is the Word of God, the division into chapters and verses was made by man.

The reason the Bible was divided into chapters and verses was to make it easy to locate specific passages. It would be very difficult to find a passage if the books were all one long paragraph.

Unity of the Bible
When we speak of the unity of the Bible, we mean two things:

The Bible Is United in Content
Even though the Bible was written by many writers over many years, there are no contradictions. The writing of one author does not contradict any of the others.

The Bible includes discussion of hundreds of controversial subjects. (A controversial subject is one that creates different opinions when mentioned.) Yet the writers of the Bible spoke on such subjects with harmony from the first book of Genesis through the last book of Revelation. This was possible because there was really only one author: God. The writers only recorded the message under His direction and inspiration. For this reason, the content of the Bible is united.

The Bible Is United in Theme
Some people think the Bible is a collection of 66 separate books on different subjects. They do not realize that the Bible is united by a major theme. From beginning to end, the Bible reveals God's special plan. This purpose is stated in the Book of Ephesians:

He made known to us the mystery of His will, according to His kind intention which He purposed in Him with a view to an administration suitable to the fullness of the times, that is, the summing up of all things in Christ, things in the heavens and things on the earth. In Him also we have obtained an inheritance, having been predestined according to His purpose who works all things after the counsel of His will (Ephesians 1:9-11).

In the Bible, God reveals "the mystery" of His plan. That plan is the unifying theme of the Bible. It is the revelation of Jesus Christ as the Savior of sinful mankind. Jesus explained how the Old Testament centered on Him: *"Now He said to them, 'These are My words which I spoke to you while I was still with you, that all things which are written about Me in the Law of Moses and the Prophets and the Psalms must be fulfilled'"* (Luke 24:44).

With this introduction, Jesus continued and *"opened their minds to understand the Scriptures"* (Luke 24:45). What was the key Jesus gave them to understanding the Scriptures? The fact is that its major theme focused on Him: *"Thus it is written, that the Christ would suffer and rise again from the dead the third day, and that repentance for forgiveness of sins would be proclaimed in His name to all the nations, beginning from Jerusalem. You are witnesses of these things"* (Luke 24:46-48).

The Old and New Testaments both tell the story of Jesus. The Old Testament prepares us for its happening. The New Testament tells that it did happen. This unites the Bible in one major theme.

The people who looked forward to Jesus under the Old Testament were saved from their sins through faith in God's promise. Everyone who looks back to it as having been fulfilled in Jesus Christ is saved in the same way: through faith that it happened just as God promised.

Diversity of the Bible
When we speak of the "diversity" of the Bible, we mean that the Bible has variety. It records different ways in which God dealt with people and the different ways in which they responded to Him.

The Bible is written in different moods. Some portions express joy while others reflect sorrow. The Bible includes different types of writing. It contains history, poetry, prophecy, letters, adventure, parables, miracles, and love stories. Because of its variety, the Bible has been further divided into major groups of books.

Old Testament Divisions
The books of the Old Testament are divided into four major groups: Law, History, Poetry, and Prophecy.

The Books of Law
There are five books of Law in the Old Testament:
- Genesis
- Exodus
- Leviticus
- Numbers
- Deuteronomy

These books record the creation of man and the world by God and the early history of man. They tell how God raised up the nation of Israel as a people through which He could reveal Himself to the nations of the world.

These books also record the laws of God. The best known parts are the Ten Commandments (Exodus 20:3-17), the greatest of all commandments (Deuteronomy 6:5), and the second greatest commandment (Leviticus 19:18).

Open your Bible and locate the books of Law in the Old Testament. Locate the three verses mentioned in the preceding paragraph and read them. These are an example of the laws of God recorded in these books.

The Books of History
There are twelve books of history in the Old Testament:
- Joshua
- Judges
- Ruth
- 1 and 2 Samuel
- 1 and 2 Kings
- 1 and 2 Chronicles

- Ezra
- Nehemiah
- Esther

Locate these books in your Bible. They are found right after the books of Law. The books of history cover a thousand-year history of God's people, Israel. Naturally they do not tell everything that happened, but they record the major events. They show the results of both following and ignoring God's law.

The Books of Poetry
There are five books of poetry in the Old Testament:
- Job
- Psalms
- Proverbs
- Ecclesiastes
- Song of Solomon

These books are the worship books of God's people, Israel. They still are used in worship by believers today. Turn to Psalm 23 and read it. This is an example of the beautiful, worship poetry contained in these books.

The Books of Prophecy
The books of prophecy in the Old Testament are divided into two groups which are called Major and Minor prophetical books. This does not mean the Major Prophets are more important than the Minor Prophets. The title is used because the Major Prophets are longer than the Minor Prophets. There are five Major Prophets in the Old Testament:
- Isaiah
- Jeremiah
- Lamentations
- Ezekiel
- Daniel

There are twelve Minor Prophets in the Old Testament:
- Hosea
- Joel
- Amos
- Obadiah
- Jonah
- Micah
- Nahum
- Habakkuk
- Zephaniah
- Haggai
- Zechariah
- Malachi

These books are prophetic messages from God to His people about what would happen in the future. Many of the prophecies have already been fulfilled. Some remain to be fulfilled in the future. Find these books of prophecy in your Bible. They are the last books in the Old Testament.

New Testament Divisions
The New Testament has also been divided into four groups: Gospels, History, Letters, and Prophecy.

The Gospels
There are four books in the Gospels:
- Matthew
- Mark
- Luke
- John

These books tell about the life, death, and resurrection of Jesus. Their purpose is to lead you to believe that He is the Christ, the Son of God. John 20:31 states this purpose. Find the Gospels in your Bible. Turn to John 20:31 and read this verse.

The Book of History
There is one book of history in the New Testament: Acts. This book tells how the church began and fulfilled Christ's commission to spread the gospel throughout the world. Locate this book in your Bible.

Letters
There are twenty-one letters in the New Testament:
- Romans
- 1 and 2 Corinthians
- Galatians
- Ephesians
- Philippians
- Colossians
- 1 and 2 Thessalonians
- 1 and 2 Timothy
- Titus
- Philemon
- Hebrews
- James
- 1 and 2 Peter
- 1, 2, and 3 John
- Jude

The letters are addressed to all believers. Their purpose is to guide them in living and help them do what Jesus commanded. Romans 12 is a good example of their teaching. Turn to this chapter in your Bible and read it.

The letters are also sometimes called "epistles." The word *epistles* means "letters."

Prophecy
There is one book of prophecy in the New Testament: Revelation. This book of prophecy tells of the final victory of Jesus and His people. Its purpose is to encourage you to keep living as Christians should live until the end of the world. Its message is summarized in Revelation 2:10. Read this verse in your Bible.

TWO

VERSIONS OF THE BIBLE

Objectives
Upon completion of this chapter you will be able to:
- Write the key verse from memory
- Name the three languages in which the Bible was written
- Define the word *version*
- Explain the difference between a translation and a paraphrase of the Bible

Key Verse
The Lord gives the command; The women who proclaim the good tidings are a great host (Psalms 68:11).

Introduction
This chapter identifies the original languages in which the Bible was written and explains how the Scriptures have been translated into other languages. You will learn the difference between a translation and a paraphrase version of the Bible. Examples from various versions of the Bible are provided.

If you do not have a Bible, this chapter will explain how to obtain one in your language.

Three Languages

The Bible was originally written in three languages. Most of the Old Testament was written in Hebrew, except for parts of the Books of Daniel and Nehemiah, which were written in Aramaic. The New Testament was written in Greek.

Unless you speak one of these three languages, the Bible was not originally written in your language. None of the original manuscripts of the Bible are now in existence. Some good manuscripts exist, which are copies of the original. Versions are translations of these copies of the original manuscripts.

From early times men saw the necessity of translating the Bible so everyone could read it in their own language. No translation is exact because no two languages are exactly alike. Some words used in the Bible do not even exist in different languages.

For example, there is a tribe of Indians in Ecuador, South America, called the Auca Indians. When missionaries first contacted them, these Indians did not know how to read or write. There were no words in their language for "writing" or "book." The Auca Indians did have a custom of carving identification marks on their property. Since there were no words in their language for "scriptures," "writing," or "book," when the Bible was translated for them it was called "God's Carving." This identified it as something belonging to God. This is an example of the difficulty of translating the Bible into various languages.

Translations and Paraphrases

There are many different versions of the Bible. The word *version* means "a Bible written in a language different from those in which God's Word was originally written." There are two main types of versions of the Bible: translations and paraphrases.

Translation

A translation is an effort to express what the Greek, Hebrew, and Aramaic words actually say. It gives as nearly as possible a literal translation for each word in the Bible. It is a word-by-word translation. Additions are

28

made only when it is necessary in order for the reader to make sense out of the meaning.

Paraphrase

A paraphrase does not attempt to translate word for word. It translates thought by thought. A paraphrase is a restatement of the meaning of a passage. Paraphrase versions are easier to read and understand because they are written in more modern vocabulary and grammar. But they are not an exact translation of God's Word.

In the "For Further Study" section of this chapter, we have provided examples from several English versions of the Bible for you to compare. These will give you an idea of the differences in translation and paraphrase versions.

Selecting a Study Bible

For the purposes of this course and Bible study in general, we recommend use of the New American Standard Version of the Bible.

Red Letter Editions

Several versions of the Bible come in what is called "red letter editions." In red letter editions of the Bible, all the words of Jesus are printed in red. The rest of the text of the Bible is printed in black ink. If a red letter edition of the New American Standard Version is available in your language, we suggest you obtain it. What Jesus taught is one of the major focuses of your training. A red letter edition emphasizes His teachings.

For Further Study

We have selected the text of John 3:16 to illustrate the differences between the various versions of the Bible. The versions listed are the most popular English versions of the Bible.

King James Version
For God so loved the world that He gave his only begotten Son, that whosoever believeth in Him should not perish but have everlasting life.

New King James Version
For God so loved the world that He gave His only begotten Son, that whoever believes in Him should not perish but have everlasting life.

Revised Standard Version -
For God so loved the world that He gave His only Son, that whoever believes in Him should not perish but have eternal life.

Living Bible Version — Dios habla hay
For God loved the world so much that He gave His only Son so that anyone who believes in Him shall not perish but have eternal life.

New American Standard Version — Biblia de Americas
For God so loved the world, that He gave His only begotten Son, that whoever believes in Him should not perish, but have eternal life.

New English Bible Version
God Loved the world so much that He gave His only Son, that everyone who has faith in Him may not die but have eternal life.

Amplified Version
For God so greatly loved and dearly prized the world that He (even) gave up His only-begotten (unique) Son, so that whoever believes in (trusts, clings to, relies on) Him shall not perish-come to destruction, be lost-but have eternal (everlasting) life.

Phillips Version
For God loved the world so much that He gave His only Son, so that everyone who believes in Him should not be lost, but should have eternal life.

Wurst Version
For in such a manner did God love the world, insomuch that His Son, the uniquely-begotten One, He gave, in order that everyone who places his trust in Him may not perish but may be having life eternal.

Berkeley Version in Modern English
For God so loved the world that He gave His only begotten Son, so that whoever believes on Him should not perish but have eternal life.

Moffat Version
For God loved the world so dearly that He gave up His only Son, so that everyone who believes in Him may have eternal life instead of perishing.

Jerusalem Bible
Yes, God loved the world so much that He gave His only Son so that everyone who believes in Him may not be lost but may have eternal life.

THREE

BIBLE BACKGROUND

Objectives
Upon completion of this chapter you will be able to:
- Write the key verse from memory
- Define "Biblical geography"
- Identify major historical periods of the Bible
- Describe everyday life in Bible times
- Define "Biblical archaeology"
- Identify when a book of the Bible was written

Key Verse
But do not let this one fact escape your notice, beloved, that with the Lord one day is like a thousand years, and a thousand years like one day (2 Peter 3:8).

Introduction
This chapter discusses the history and geography of the Bible and everyday life in Bible times. It also provides the date when each book of the Bible was written.

Biblical Geography

Geography is the study and description of the earth, its land, political and natural boundaries, and bodies of water. Biblical geography is the study of the land where events in the Bible occurred.

Chronological History

God functions in the realm of eternity. He is not governed by the earthly concept of time: *"But do not let this one fact escape your notice, beloved, that with the Lord one day is like a thousand years, and a thousand years like one day."* (2 Peter 3:8).

Man, however, functions in the realm of the earthly concept of time. Chronological history tells when an event occurred in the past. *Chronological* means "in order or sequence." Chronological history organizes events of the past in proper order.

In most of the world the dating of time is divided into two major periods. These two periods are shown by the use of initials before or after the number of the year. The initials BC mean an event happened before the birth of Christ. The initials AD mean an event happened after the time of the birth of Christ. Thus, when we say something happened 250 BC, it means it happened 250 years before Christ. When we say an event happened 700 AD, it means it happened 700 years after the birth of Christ.

When a number has BC after it, the larger the number is the older the date is. When a number has AD after it, the larger the number is, the more recently the event occurred. For example, 500 BC is older than 500 AD because it occurred 500 years before Christ, while 500 AD occurred 500 years after Christ.

There are several ways we are able to know the chronological history of Bible events. For some events, the Bible itself provides the date. With other events, the early writings of historians provide dates. Also, dates can be determined through archaeology. Archaeology is the study of ancient things. It is a science which gains knowledge of times past from the study of existing remains of their civilizations. (Biblical archaeology is the study of remains found in Bible lands. Some of the historical record of the Bible has been gained by dating these remains.)

Chronological History of the Bible

1. Creation to Abraham: From Creation to 2000 BC
The creation of the universe, the fall of man into sin, the murder of Abel by Cain, Noah and the flood, and the Tower of Babel are some of the major Bible events of this period.

2. Abraham to Moses: 200 - 1500 BC
The experience of one man, Abraham, and his descendants are the focus of this period. From Abraham, God raised up the nation of Israel through which He wanted to reveal Himself to the nation of the world. This period includes the stories of Isaac, the son of Abraham, and of Isaac's son, Jacob. The period climaxes with the story of Joseph, Jacob's son, who was sold into slavery in Egypt and became a great ruler. Jacob and his family later joined Joseph in Egypt.

3. The Exodus: 1500 - 1460 BC
Between the close of Genesis and the opening of Exodus, approximately 100 years passed. The family of Jacob multiplied into the nation of Israel in Egypt during this time.

The Egyptians became fearful because of the rapid increase of the Israelites, so they made them slaves. Moses was raised up, and under his leadership the Israelites miraculously departed from Egypt.

After spending a year at Mt. Sinai, they wandered for thirty-eight years in the desert. This period closed with the death of Moses and the leadership of Israel being assumed by a man named Joshua.

4. The Conquest of Canaan: 1460 - 1450 BC
During this period, Joshua led Israel into Canaan to possess the land God had promised them. When the ungodly people of this area were conquered militarily, the land was divided among the twelve tribes of Israel. This period of ten years is recorded in the Book of Joshua.

5. The Judges: 1450 - 1102 BC
This was a time during which God raised up judges to rule the people of Israel. It is a dark period of time in the story of Israel, as it was a time of

spiritual failure. This period lasted for 348 years.

6. *The Kingdom: 1102 - 986 BC*
Samuel, the last judge of Israel, established a kingdom of Israel and anointed Saul to be king. Three kings, Saul, David, and Solomon each reigned about forty years.

During this time the nation of Israel attained the highest glory in their history. The government was firmly established and Israel's borders were expanded. The story of this period, as well as the three following periods, are recorded in 1 and 2 Samuel, 1 and 2 Kings, and 1 and 2 Chronicles. The kingdom period lasted for 120 years and then the kingdom was divided.

7. *The Two Kingdoms: 982 - 722 BC*
When the evil son of Solomon, Rehoboam, came to the throne, the northern tribes revolted. They established a separate kingdom of Israel. The kingdom in the south became known as the kingdom of Judah. For about 259 years Israel was divided into these two kingdoms.

8. *Judah Alone: 722 - 587 BC*
Israel, the Northern Kingdom, was conquered by the Assyrians in 722 BC. The people were taken captive into Assyria. After the fall of Israel, the Southern Kingdom of Judah lasted 135 years. Judah's kings had shown more loyalty to God and the people had not gone so deep in sin.

9. *The Captivity: 587 - 538 BC*
In spite of the warnings of the prophets, Judah finally went deeper into sin until God gave them over to be conquered by Nebuchadnezzar and taken captive into Babylon.

The city of Jerusalem was destroyed and the people of God, who a few hundred years before had miraculously crossed the Jordan River, now marched away in chains.

36

10. The Restoration: 538 - 391 BC

When a king by the name of Cyrus became leader of Babylon, he permitted God's people to return and rebuild Jerusalem and their temple of worship. Zerubbabel led the group who returned to reestablish themselves in the promised land. The records of this period are found in the Books of Ezra, Nehemiah, and Esther. This period of restoration lasted for 147 years.

Between the Testament: 391 - 5 BC

The Old Testament closes with Israel back in Canaan. Then came a period of about 400 years between the Old Testament and New Testament. There were no Bible books written during this period so information on the time comes only from secular writings.

During this time Palestine was ruled by the Persians (536 -333 BC), the Greeks (333 - 323 BC), the Egyptians (323 - 204 BC), the Syrians (204 - 165 BC), the Maccabeans (165 - 63 BC), and Rome (63 BC through the time of Christ).

11. Life of Christ: 5 BC to 28 AD

After 400 years, John the Baptist was raised up by God to prepare the way for the coming of Jesus Christ. Jesus was to be the Savior of sinful mankind. The promise of this plan of salvation was first made in the garden of Eden when man originally sinned (Genesis 3:15).

Jesus was miraculously born of a virgin, revealed Himself to Israel as the Messiah, was rejected, crucified for the sins of all mankind, and resurrected by the power of God. Matthew, Mark, Luke, and John record this period of thirty-three years.

12. The Spread Of The Gospel: 28 - 100 AD

This period covers the events after the life of Jesus and His return to heaven following His resurrection. It records the spread of the gospel from Jerusalem to Judea, Samaria, and the uttermost parts of the world.

Life in Bible Times

The Bible, historians, and archaeological studies have provided information on the everyday life of people in Bible times. Prior to the time when they went to Egypt, the people of Israel lived in tents. They moved about with their flocks and herds in search of fresh pasture and water.

After the exodus from Egypt and the years traveling in the desert, the Israelites settled in their promised land of Canaan. From that time on, the life of the oridinary people followed a pattern that changed little throughout the years.

Peasent men worked either in the fields or in a village craft while the women and children kept the home. Farming and shepherding were both important occupations. There was some fishing and all kinds of village crafts, including carpentry, pottery, and leather work.

Water was in short supply since the land was hot and dry for most of the year. Water was drawn from a village well in a goatskin bucket. This was an important place of socializing for the women.

People wore long flowing robes in order to keep cool. The material of the robe was decided by wealth. The wealthy could afford brightly-dyed cloth. Often clothes indicated a man's profession. For example, the priests wore special clothing and the rabbi (religious leader of Israel) wore a blue-fringed robe. Shoes were made of cow hide soles with leather thongs which fastened to the ankle.

Marriages were arranged by parents, and there was little social mixing between young people. Because the bride was a working asset, she had to be paid for with a bride price. Domestic life centered in the home.

In Old Testament times there was no school for common men's children. They were taught everyday skills and religion by their parents. By the time of Jesus, a girl's education was still entirely her mother's responsibility. Boys went to a school at the synagogue from age six on. The Old Testament was the textbook they used to learn the history, geography, literature, and law. Exceptional students were sent to Jerusalem to learn from the rabbis. Each boy also had to learn a trade.

When a boy was thirteen years old, he became *Bar Mitzvah,* which is Jewish for "a son of the Law." This meant that he was considered to be a man.

Death among the people of Israel called for elaborate ceremonies of mourning. Sometimes professional mourners would be hired to weep. In New Testament times bodies were anointed and wrapped in special grave clothes. Poor people were buried in common graves or caves, but the wealthy had tombs dug out of rocks and sealed with a flat boulder.

There was no division between civil and religious law in Israel. The gate of the city or village was the place where problems were formally judged. The highest court in New Testament times was the Sanhedrin which consisted of seventy men who met in the temple. The Roman authorities, who were in control of Israel during New Testament times, allowed the Israelites to pass any sentence under their law except the death penalty.

The religious life of Israel centered first on the tabernacle and later on the temple in Jerusalem. The Old Testament religious regulations were administered by the priests and the Levites. The greatest religious day of the year was the Day of Atonement. On this day the high priest entered the innermost room of the temple to make atonement for his own sins and the sins of the people.

Other festivals included the Passover, which was a way of remembering Israel's escape from Egypt. The Feast of Pentecost marked the beginning of harvest, and the Feast of Tabernacles was the harvest festival. The Feast of Purim recalled Esther's deliverance of Israel, and the Feast of Trumpets marked the start of the new year.

Between the end of the Old Testament and the beginning of the New Testament, regular worship shifted from the main temple to the local synagogue. This practice started in the days when Israel was in captivity and there was no temple in Jerusalem.

Only men took an active part in the synagogue service. The women and children sat in a different section. The pattern of the service included statement of a creed, prayers, and readings from the Law and prophets. This was followed by a sermon and a time when the men could question the minister. The Old Testament Scriptures were contained on sacred scrolls which only the doctors of law might open.

The story of the Bible is set against this background of traditional family and rural life, which did not change for centuries. It was also set against the background of warring empires around Israel and the influence of the Roman Empire. Rome had extended to control Israel during the time of Jesus.

When the Books Were Written

The books of the Bible are not arranged in chronological order. This means they are not arranged in the order in which they were written. Bible scholars have used information from two sources to determine the dates when books were written. First, the Bible sometimes refers to historical events that help date the writing. An example of this is Luke's mention of government officials by name (Luke 3:1). Also, there were many early secular writings by historians and philosophers, which referenced events mentioned in the Bible.

The following list is arranged in chronological order according to the most probable dates the various books were written:

Old Testament

Book	Date BC
Genesis	1400
Exodus	1400
Leviticus	1400
Numbers	1400
Deuteronomy	1400
Joshua	1235
Judges	1025
1 Samuel	1000 - 850
2 Samuel	1000 - 850
1 Kings	970 - 850
Psalms	970 - 440
Ecclesiastes	962 - 922
Song of Solomon	962 - 922

Job	900
Proverbs	900
2 Kings	850 - 586
Obadiah	848 - 841
Joel	835 - 796
Jonah	780 - 750
Amos	765 - 750
Hosea	755 - 715
Isaiah	750 - 680
Micah	740 - 690
Jeremiah	640 - 586
Lamentations	640 - 586
Nahum	630 - 612
Habakkuk	625
Zephaniah	621
Ezekiel	593 - 571
Haggai	520
Zechariah	520 - 515
Zechariah 9 - 14	After 500
Esther	486 - 465
Nehemiah	445
Malachi	433 - 400
Ezra	400
Ruth	399 - 300
1 Chronicles	350
2 Chronicles	350
Ecclesiastes	175

New Testament

Book	Date AD
James	45
Mark	50
1 Thessalonians	51 - 52
2 Thessalonians	51 - 52
1 Corinthians	54 - 55

2 Corinthians	55 - 56
Galatians	55 - 56
Romans	56 - 58
Luke	58 - 63
Ephesians	61 - 62
Philippians	61 - 62
Philemon	62
Colossians	62 - 63
Acts	63
1 Peter	64
1 Timothy	64
2 Timothy	64
Titus	64
2 Peter	66
Hebrews	68
Matthew	75
1 John	85 - 90*
John	90 - 100*
Jude	90 - 125*
Revelation	90 - 95*
2 John	96*
3 John	97*

* Date in dispute. Many believe they were written prior to the fall of Jerusalem in AD 70.

For Further Study

1. If you are interested in Bible chronology, *The Narrated Bible*, published by Harvest House Publishers, Eugene, Oregon, is a good tool for chronological study of the Bible. This book does not give the actual Bible text, but provides Bible references in chronological order and a brief narrative (commentary) on each reference.

2. If you are interested in Biblical archaeology, the following books are suggested:

Beginnings in Biblical Archaeology by Howard Vos, published by Moody Press, Chicago, Illinois, USA.

Archaeology in Bible Lands by Howard Vos, published by Moody Press, Chicago, Illinois, USA

FOUR

AN INTRODUCTION TO OUTLINING

Objectives
Upon completion of this chapter you will be able to:
- Write the key verse from memory
- Define the term *outline*
- Read an outline
- Create an outline

Key Verse
Moreover, He said to me, "Son of man, take into your heart all My words which I will speak to you and listen closely" (Ezekiel 3:10).

Introduction
This course, "Journey Through The New Testament," includes an outline of each book of the Bible. The outlines provide an overview of the general content of God's Word.

More detailed outlines are given in *Part Two for the Gospels, Acts, and the Epistles* due to the special focus of Harvestime International Institute. The Institute emphasizes what Jesus taught and the results when His teachings were put into action in the early church.

The outlines in this course summarize only the general content of each book of the Bible. When you complete this general survey, you should go back and study each book in more detail. The outlines in this course are a starting point for you to develop more detailed outlines of each book of the Bible. To do this, you must know how to create a proper outline.

Outlining

An outline is a method of organizing study notes. It puts information in summary form for use in future ministry and study. An outline helps you "hear with your ear and receive in your heart" the Word of God (Ezekiel 3:10).

An outline centers on a selected subject. This subject becomes the title of the outline. We have used the names of Bible books as outline titles in this course because they are the subjects of study.

The main points in the outline tell something about the subject. There are also sub-points which tell something about main points. The prefix "sub" means they relate to (tell something about) the main point. They provide more detailed information about the main points.

There are many ways to outline. We have selected one which uses special numbers called Roman numerals for the main points. If you are not familiar with Roman numerals, a list is provided in the "For Further Study" section of this chapter. Subpoints on the outline are shown with capital letters of the alphabet. If there are further points under these, they are shown with regular numbers.

Study the following example of an outline:

The Title Is Placed Here

I. This is the Roman numeral for 1 used for the first main point.
    A. This is a capital letter used for a subpoint relating to the main point.
        1. If there was a further subpoint relating to this, it would be marked with the number 1.
        2. If there are other points relating back to subpoint A, continue to place them in numerical order.

B. Next sub pont. I may have several subpoints. If so, continue down through the alphabet using capital letters in order. Each one of these should relate to the main point.
II. To present another main point, use the next Roman numeral.
  A. Subpoints follow the same pattern under every main point.

Expanding the Outlines
As an example of how you can expand the general outlines given in this course, we have selected Romans 12:1-2. First read the verses:
  Therefore I urge you, brethren, by the mercies of God, to present your bodies a living and holy sacrifice, acceptable to God, which is your spiritual service of worship. And do not be conformed to this world, but be transformed by the renewing of your mind, so that you may prove what the will of God is, that which is good and acceptable and perfect.

Here is the outline developed from the verses:

Steps for Finding God's Will
I. Present your bodies a living sacrifice:
  A. Holy
  B. Acceptable unto God
II. Be not conformed to this world:
  A. Be transformed.
    1. We are transformed by the renewing of our minds.
III. These steps will help us prove or find the will of God which is:
  A. Good
  B. Acceptable
  C. Perfect

You can see how this outline clearly summarizes the steps to God's will given in Romans 12:1-2. You will never complete your outline study of God's Word. The Holy Spirit will constantly give you new understanding about the Word, which you will want to add to your outlines.

PART 2
THE NEW TESTAMENT

FIVE

PRELIMINARIES TO THE GOSPELS

Each of the Gospels are unique in their style and purpose of their message. The Gospels contain the primary sayings, history, and story of the life of our Lord and Savior Jesus Christ. When I say that each one is unique, you will see that the Gospels portray a certain aspect or picture of Jesus, who He was, and His role within the viewpoint of the Gospel writer. Further you will see that each writer is writing their Gospel to a certain audience so that they might understand clearly that Jesus Christ is the Messiah, the Son of the living God.

As we begin the New Testament, it is important to recognize that there has been a 400 year period since any true prophetic message or any written Scriptures. During that time many events occurred, but primarily it was a waiting period, looking forward to the time of the coming Messiah. It was a time of great political unrest. The children of God no longer had a viable spiritual life. They had primarily become politically and religiously oriented. It was a time when the Roman government overshadowed all of the people of God. It was a time when many were looking for a deliverer, a conqueror, a king that would restore back to Israel the splendor that they had enjoyed during the reign of King David and King Solomon.

This was the world that Jesus came into. As we will see in the Gospel stories, Jesus came, as a lowly, meek, and mild babe in a manger, growing up in a Jewish home, prepared to be a Jewish citizen within a Roman state. He became a young man and a man of full age, operating in great power and controversy, a teacher, a rabbi, a miracle worker, a mystery, eventually to become the Savior of the world.

The new covenant that Jesus came to present did not negate the important aspects of the law but fulfilled all that God had intended so that man could become all that God created him to be.

As we look into the Gospels and then into the Acts of the Apostles and the letters written to the church, it is with a great sense of awe and of wonderment because of the great things that God has done.

SIX

Written to the Jews

MATTHEW

Introduction

The Book of Matthew, which was written by Matthew, also called Levi, one of the twelve Apostles to the Jews, portrays Jesus as the great Messianic King.

Contained in this book is the primary mission of Christ, and it utilizes the key words which were frequently repeated to indicate that Christ had fulfilled the Old Testament prophecies concerning Himself (the kingdom of heaven is at hand).

Some of the distinct features of the Book of Matthew include the complete genealogy of Christ, showing that He was in line to become the Jewish King, and many passages (including certain parables and miracles) that are contained only in the Gospel of Matthew.

The primary focus of this Gospel, as mentioned earlier, is to see Jesus Christ as the great Messianic King, as the Son of David, as the One who had the right to sit upon the throne of David. Yet, Jesus was more than just a political king. He was a spiritual King and Savior.

You can see in the context of Matthew's Gospel the attempt to link the two great covenants that God made between His people, the Davidic and the Abrahamic covenant. He shows that both were completely fulfilled in Christ. Further, we see that the kingdom of heaven has come, and that Christ is truly the One to reign on David's throne, over a kingdom not of this world, but a kingdom that will never end.

Jesus: The Messianic King

1. Matthew was written primarily to the Jews, and secondarily to all mankind.

2. A primary purpose for the book is to show the Jews that Jesus is the long-expected Messiah (Matthew 1:1).

3. Jesus Christ is presented as the "Son of David." He is rightfully a "king." His royal genealogy is given in chapter one.

4. The prophets had prophesied of the kingly office of the Messiah: Psalm 72; Isaiah 6-7, 32:1; Jeremiah 23:5; Zechariah 9:9, 14:9.

5. Pictures in Matthew's Gospel which particularly portray Jesus as the "King" include: the wise men, John the Baptist, the Sermon on the Mount, the Transfiguration, the Crucifixion, and the open tomb.

6. The "King" gives the Royal Manifesto in His Sermon on the Mount (chapters 5-7). Here is contained the laws of His kingdom.

7. Matthew is concerned with the coming of a promised Savior. The Jew was steeped in the Old Testament Scriptures. He must know that this Jesus came to fulfill the prophecies of the Old Testament.

8. Matthew's Gospel attempts to link the two great covenants that God made with His covenant people: the Davidic covenant and the Abrahamic covenant. Matthew shows that Christ fulfilled both of these covenants.
   a. Davidic Covenant: God had promised that David would never lack a man to sit upon his throne (2 Samuel 7:5-17).
   b. Abrahamic Covenant: God had promised that in a descendant of Abraham, all the families of the earth should be blessed (Genesis 12:1-3).
   c. Thus, Matthew opens with the birth of a King, and closes with the offering of a Sacrifice. David's son was a king; Abraham's son was a sacrifice.

9. A key expression is "the kingdom of heaven," found only in the Gospel of Matthew. This expression is a Hebraism evidently taken from Daniel's prophecy (2:44), which prophesies that the God of heaven shall set up a kingdom.

Outline
I. The Coming of the King (1:1-2:23)
II. The Proclamation of the Kingdom (3:1-16:20)
III. The Rejection of the King (16:21-20:34)
IV. The Triumph of the King (21:1-28:20)

SEVEN

MARK

Written to Romans (handwritten annotation)

Introduction

Mark was the son of Mary of Jerusalem, also referred to as John Mark, a relative of Barnabus, and one that was associated with Paul and Barnabus in Paul and Barnabus' first missionary journey. He was the one that was temporarily alienated from the Apostle Paul in Acts 13:13-15.

In the Book of Mark you see a slightly different emphasis. It is primarily written to the Romans, and depicts Jesus as the servant of the Lord. The primary purpose of this Gospel is to show to the mind of the Roman citizen that Jesus had every right to be the ultimate leader because He was the ultimate servant.

Mark contains an emphasis on Jesus' deeds more than His words. The Romans cared very little for the words of a man but cared a great deal for his deeds. In fact, it is in Mark that we see the Roman centurion speaking that Christ must have been the Son of God. The Roman showed great respect for one who was willing to lay down his life for a greater cause.

Finally we see in the Gospel of Mark the ministry of Christ as a servant, that He was filled with wisdom, labored faithfully, that He had authority, majesty, and faithfulness in all that He did. Mark's concern was to depict Christ as a powerful, overcoming, authoritative Savior shown by His actions more than by His words.

Jesus: The Servant of the Lord

1. This Gospel was written primarily to the Romans, and secondarily to all mankind. The Roman of Jesus' day was like the average businessman or laborer of today. He is not so concerned about a "king's" business but a God who is "able" to meet man's every need.

2. The primary purpose is to record more of Jesus' deeds than His words (Mark 10:45). Thus more miracles are recorded here than in any other Gospel. More verbs of action are recorded than in any other Gospel. The Romans cared very little for words but far more for deeds.

3. There is no genealogy of Jesus. Men may be interested in the genealogy of a king (Matthew) but not of a servant.

4. The prophets had prophesied of the office of the Messiah as One who would be a servant: Isaiah 42:1-7; 52:13-15; 53.

5. Pictures in Mark's Gospel which particularly portray Jesus as a servant include: the baptism of Jesus, the draught of fishes, the calling of the Twelve, Jairus' daughter healed, Jesus walking on the sea.

6. The manner in which Christ served as a servant:
   a. In humility (Mark 1:36-38, 44; 3:6-12; 7:36)
   b. In tenderness (Mark 1:30-31; 9:27; 10:13-16)
   c. Amidst opposition (Mark 2:1-12; 3:1-5; 5:40; 8:11)
   d. In self-sacrifice (Mark 3:20; 6:31, 53-56)
   e. In love (Mark 1:41; 5:21-43; 8:1-9; 10:21)
   f. In prayerfulness (Mark 9:14-29; 14:32-42)

7. The ministry of Christ as a servant:
   a. With Wisdom: He not only labored faithfully Himself, but He selected and prepared others for work (Mark 1:14-20; 2:13, 14; 3:14-19; 4:7-13)
   b. With Authority: Because He was under the Father's authority, He could exercise authority. He had power over demons, elements, and

death (Mark 1:21-28; 4:35-41; 5:1-43; 6:47-51; 9:14-29)

c. With Majesty: He was not man's servant but God's servant (Mark 11:1-33)

d. With Faithfulness: His service was up to the last hour (Mark 14, 15)

8. Mark is concerned with the life of a powerful Savior.

Outline

I. Preparation of the Servant (1:1-13)

II. The Labor of the Servant (1:14-8:30)

III. The Rejection of the Servant (8:31-15:57)

IV. The Exaltation of the Servant (16:1-20)

EIGHT

Written to Greeks

LUKE

Introduction

The Gospel of Luke was written by Luke, the beloved physician. He was also the writer of the Book of Acts. Luke was addressed to Theophilus, who was an unknown person of apparently Greek origin, clearly a Gentile.

The major theme of the Gospel is the universal grace of God and its emphasis on the Son of Man, depicting Christ as the perfect man. One of the primary things that Greek students and idealists would seek was that of truth. Truth could only be found in a perfect or ideal man shown clearly by Luke. Christ was that ideal man.

In this Gospel there is also a devotional theme. There is a powerful emphasis on prayer, with a note of joy and praise in it. Secondly, it honors womanhood. Thirdly, quite significantly it is a biography of Christ Himself.

Luke's primary emphasis is on the humanity of Christ. We see Christ expressing feelings and involved the mentality of His ministry. It's a very powerful book, showing the Son of Man as that perfect man, the only One that could provide salvation and a way for us to live, whereby we become all that God created us to be.

Jesus: The Son of Man

1. This Gospel was written primarily to the Greeks, and secondarily to all mankind.

2. The primary purpose is to reach mankind where he is in his sin (Luke 19:10). This is the Gospel for the sinner.

3. Portraying Jesus as the "perfect man," Luke's genealogy goes back to Adam, the first man.

4. The prophets had prophesied that the Messiah would be a "Son of Man" (Genesis 3:15, 22:18; Isaiah 7:14-16, 9:6).

5. Pictures in Luke's Gospel which particularly portray Jesus as the "Perfect Man" include: the visit of the shepherds, the birth of Jesus, the boy Jesus, the parable of the sower, the good Samaritan, the lost sheep, the little children blessed, the rich young ruler, the penitent thief, and the Ascension.

6. In Luke's Gospel, the humanity of Christ's incarnation is emphasized. Luke gives the fullest particulars concerning the virgin birth of Jesus. He is shown as toiling with His hands, weeping over the city, kneeling in prayer, suffering in agony. Five out of the six miracles in the Gospel were miracles of physical healing.

7. Luke's Gospel seems to concentrate on the "outcast" of the earth. So it is Luke who records the Good Samaritan (10:33), the publican (18:13), Zacchaeus (19:2), and the thief on the cross (23:43). Luke says also the most about women and children: 8:42; 9:38; 7:46; 8:3; 11:27; 10:38-42; 23:27.

8. As a book of Christ's humanity, we see more than in any other book the exercising of Jesus' spiritual man. More than any other Gospel, we see Christ praying: at His baptism (3:2-10), alone (5:16), all night (6:12), on the mountain (9:28-29), His exemplary prayer (11:1-4), for His friends (22:31-32), in the garden (22:41-42), and on the cross (23:34).

Outline

I. The Perfect Man in Preparation (1:1-4:13)
II. The Perfect Man in Ministry (4:14-19:48)
III. The Perfect Man in Suffering (20:1-23:56)
IV. The Perfect Man in Victory (24:1-53)

NINE

JOHN

introduces Him

Introduction

The fourth Gospel, the Gospel of John, depicts Jesus as the Son of God. This is every man's Gospel. It was not written to any specific group, as the other three Gospels were, but is written primarily to the totality of mankind.

John's primary concern in his Gospel is the possession of a personal Savior. His purpose was to write this Gospel to inspire faith in Jesus Christ as the Son of God. It is by far the deepest and the most spiritual book found in the Bible. It gives a greater revelation of Christ Himself and God the Father through the "I Am" spoken throughout this book.

The revelation of the deity of Christ can be found in no other book like the Gospel of John. From the incarnation, through the private ministry, to the victory of death, we see the depiction of Christ as that perfect Son of God in total obedience to His Father. There are two great currents of thought that seem to flow throughout this book. They are faith and eternal life, that through faith in the Lord Jesus Christ, eternal life can be found for each individual. There is a very intimate and personal look at Jesus as the Christ in personal relationships with His disciples in a way that all Christians hope to obtain.

In terms of faith, Christ was the most faithful of all. In His faithfulness He ministered to His disciples. In His faithfulness He cared for the needs of the people. In His faithfulness He was willing to receive the poor and the outcasts. And in faithfulness He submitted even unto death. He faced the cross, triumphing over it through the resurrection and ultimately His ascension to His throne at the right hand of the Father.

In terms of eternal life, Jesus was the incarnate Word. He was eternal from the beginning, willing to empty Himself and lay down His divinity to take on humanity, that He might experience the totality of that humanity, and that He might be able to present to all people the opportunity to taste of the eternal life that He has always had with His Father.

Of course, one of the most beloved Scriptures is John 3:16: *"For God so loved the world, that He gave His only begotten Son, that whoever believes in Him shall not perish, but have eternal life."* Jesus came as the Great "I Am," God in a body, to bring eternal life to all of mankind. In John's Gospel, more then in any other writings, perhaps, you will see eternal life through the faithful Savior, Jesus, the Son of God presented for us all.

Jesus: The Son of God

1. This Gospel is written generally to all mankind. The "all men" of Judah's day were much like the masses of today.

2. The primary purpose of the Gospel is that men might believe that Jesus is the Christ and be led to Him (John 20:31).

3. The key word of the Gospel is *believe* (98 times).

4. The prophets had portrayed the Messiah as One who would be fully God: Isaiah 9:6, 40:3-5, 47:4; Jeremiah 23:6.

5. Pictures in John's Gospel which particularly portray Jesus as the Son of God include: Jesus and the Samaritan woman, healing of the nobleman's son, Jesus and Nicodemus, the True Vine, the feeding of the 5,000, the Great Physician, the Good Shepherd, the Light of the World, the triumphant entry, the Last Supper, and Jesus in Gethsemane.

6. The Revelation of His Deity in John's Gospel:
   a. He speaks of God as "My Father" (35 times).
   b. He speaks with absolute authority. He says, "Verily, verily" (25 times).
   c. His titles in the Gospel are those of deity. Only here is He called "the Word," called "the Creator," called the "only begotten of the Father," and called "the Lamb of God"
   d. His revelation as the Great "I AM" (see Exodus 3:14). Seven-fold witness:
   • I AM the bread of life (6:35)
   • I AM the light of the world (8:12)
   • Before Abraham was, I AM (8:58)
   • I AM the good Shepherd (10:11)
   • I AM the resurrection and the life (11:25)
   • I AM the way, the truth, and the life (14:6)
   • I AM the true vine (15:1)
   e. A seven-fold affirmation of His deity:
   • John the Baptist, "This is the Son of God" (1:34)
   • Nathaniel, "Thou art the Son of God" (1:49)
   • Peter, "Thou art the Son of God" (1:49)
   • Peter, "Thou art that Christ, the Son of the living God (6:69)
   • Martha, "Thou art the Christ, the Son of God" (11:27)
   • Thomas, "My Lord and my God" (20:28)
   • John, "Jesus is the Christ, the Son of God" (20:31)
   • Christ Himself, "I am the Son of God" (10:36).

7. John is concerned with the possession of a personal Savior.

Outline (The outline is contained within the passage of 16:28)
I. The Incarnation of God, "I came forth from the Father" (1:1-18)
II. The Parable Ministry, "And am come into the world" (1:19-12:50)
III. The Private Ministry, "Again I leave the world" (Ch. 13-19)
IV. The Victory over Death, "And go to the Father" (Ch. 20-21)

TEN

ACTS

Introduction

This book is typically known as the Acts of the Apostles, but in reality it is the Acts of the Holy Spirit through the Apostles. It shows the establishment of the church as the Apostles and those that came to know Christ as Lord and Savior went about witnessing and fulfilling the great commission that Jesus gave in Matthew 28:18.

This book was most probably written by Luke, the beloved physician, and is a sequel to the Gospel of Luke. It presents the dynamic history and the development of the early church from the ascension of Christ to Paul's imprisonment.

In the Book of Acts, we see the witnessing and the power of the Holy Spirit flowing through the Apostles and those that were raised up as deacons and elders.

Initially the church was established in the city of Jerusalem. Jerusalem was a center of commerce and religious activity for the children of Israel and the Hebrew people. But after a period of time, primarily because of the lack of fulfillment of the mandate given by Jesus Himself to go to all the world and preach the gospel, persecution came to the church and eventually the center for religious life centered in the cities of Antioch and Ephesus.

In both Jerusalem and in the cities of Antioch and Ephesus the gospel is seen being taken beyond the Hebrew people to the Gentiles and eventually to the nations of the world. This expression of the kingdom occurred through the missionary activity flowing out of the church in Antioch and the mighty miracles of the Holy Spirit.

In the Book of Acts is seen a church that is filled with the power of the Holy Spirit to witness in Jerusalem and eventually moving to Judea and Samaria and to the very uttermost parts of the earth. A tremendous explosion of the church occurred during this time with the primary characters found in the Book of Acts being the Apostle Peter and the Apostle Paul.

Witnessing

1. The primary purpose of the Book of Acts is to show how the ascended Christ continued to do His work through the Holy Spirit for the establishing of the church. A secondary purpose is to give authoritative information concerning the historical activity of the leadership and laymen of the early church as examples for us.

2. The key words in the book are *witness* (over 30 times) and *Holy Spirit* (about 70 times).

3. A characteristic feature of the Book of Acts is the recording of sermons and addresses, especially those of the Apostles. There are a total of twenty-four addresses or excerpts: nine by Peter (1:16-22; 2:14b-36; 3:15b-26; 4:8b-12; 5:29b-32; 8:20-25; 10:34b-43; 11:5-17; 15:7-11); nine also by Paul (13:16b-41; 14:15-17; 17:22b-31; 20:18b-35; 22:1-21; 24:10b-21; 26:2-23; 27:21-26; 28:17-20); and one each by James (15:15b-21), Stephen (7:2-52), Gamaliel (5:35b-39), Demetrius (19:25b-27), Festus (25:24-27), and the town clerk (19:35b-40).

4. Acts presents a graphic description of the ministry of the Holy Spirit.
   a. The baptism in the Holy Spirit and filling of the Spirit (Chapter 2; 4:23-31; 8:14-17; 10:44-48; 19:1-6)
   b. Being led by the Holy Spirit (8:29; 15:28; 16:6, 7)
   c. Judgment of sin (5:1-11)

70

d. Gifts, signs, and wonders (Ch. 2; 4:23-31; 8:14-17; 10:44-48; 19:1-6; 20:22-23; 21:11; 20:28)

7. In Acts we see the dynamics of a powerful church.
   a. A confessing church (2:4)
   b. A convicting church (2:7)
   c. A converting church (2:37)
   d. A consistent church (2:42)
   e. A contributing church (2:44-45)
   f. A communing church (2:46)
   g. A contagious church (2:47)

Outline (The outline is suggested by Acts 1:8)
I. Power for Witnessing (1:1-2:47)
II. Witnessing in Jerusalem, City Evangelism (3:1-8:3) Local
III. Witnessing in Judea and Samaria, Home Missions (8:4-12:25)
IV. Witnessing in the Uttermost Part of the Earth, Foreign Missions (Chs. 13-28)

71

ELEVEN

ROMANS

Introduction

The Apostle Paul wrote the letter to the church in Rome. This letter is broken down into two primary parts. The first part is doctrinal, clarifying teaching on God's plan for salvation. The second part is practical theology; that is, it details the life the Christian needs to live regardless of cultural background.

This book is probably the most outstanding of Paul's writings in terms of doctrinal teaching found within the Word of God. Paul masterfully presents a picture of our universal guilt and the sinful nature that we all have within us. The fact that all men must come to a personal relationship with God through His Son Jesus Christ is clearly and profoundly presented.

The outline of the plan of salvation (the method being justification or righteousness by faith, which is universal for all mankind) is clearly illustrated through the life of Abraham in his obedience and faithfulness to God. This free gift of salvation is powerful enough to eliminate even the desire for continuing sin. It shows that there is a struggle for the mind where sinful tendencies due to the lust of the flesh occur. Yet, we have power through Christ to overcome. The culmination of that wonderful divine plan is a new spiritual life of liberty. At one point we were enslaved by the law of sin and death, but now alive unto Christ, justified (made right) by the blood of our Lord and Savior Jesus Christ.

A primary theme in Romans is how faithfulness to follow after the things of God will bring a restoration of Israel. It is a promise, not just for the nation of Israel but the mystical Israel, which is the church.

In the practical aspect of the Book of Romans, we see the Apostle Paul addressing such issues as Christian duties, relationships to one another, civic and social duties, and the duty of living life in peace and harmony with self, nature, and our God. He expresses the great need for continual striving to fulfill the pattern of godly living and serving God with all of our heart.

Justification

1. This epistle was written to the saints at Rome (1:7, 15) but is intended for all men, both the Jews and Gentiles (2:1, 3, 17; 11:13). This epistle was written from Corinth about 58 AD.

2. The purpose for this epistle is general. Paul had no special errors to correct or disorders to reform as in the other epistles. Only here does Paul present doctrine in its full connection, while the other epistles seem to presuppose the knowledge of Christian doctrine. The general reasons for the epistle, however, seem to be these: (a) to teach the believers at Rome the foundational doctrines of salvation and to protect them against the error of the Judaizers (Chs. 1-8); (b) to explain the position of God regarding Israel in her unbelief (Chs. 9-11); and (c) to urge the Roman believers to enter fully into the principles of Christian living.

3. The theme is introduced in the key verses of the book, Romans 1:16-17. Here the theme is brought forth as "Justification through the righteousness of God which is attainable by all who believe."

4. The major doctrinal truths treated in the book are justification and sanctification: (a) Justification is presented as imputing to the believer the act of being clothed with the righteousness of God. The "righteousness of God" is emphasized about sixty-five times in the book; (b) Sanctification is the progressive application of the righteousness of God to the experiential life of the believer. Justification then refers to the

74

believer's standing and position before God, while sanctification deals with the daily living of God's righteousness.

5. The approach of Romans may be seen in two major divisions: (a) the first half of Romans (Chs. 1-8) deals with what God did for us; (b) the second half of Romans (Chs. 9-16) deals with what we may do with God. Consequently, the latter half of the book urges the believer to have his life measure up to his belief. The believer is saved to serve, and thus the Christian life must be lived in its proper relation to God, self, and others.

Outline
I. Doctrinal Development of What God Did for Us (Chs. 1-8)
    A. The Necessity of Justification (1:1-3:20)
    B. The Exposition of Justification (3:21-5:21)
    C. The Effects of Justification (3:21-5:21)
II. The Practical Application of God's Work to Daily Living (Chs. 9-16)
    A. How to Live a Christian Life (Chs. 9-11)
    B. How to Serve God (Chs. 12-16)

TWELVE

Discipline Letter

1 CORINTHIANS

Introduction

The Book of 1 Corinthians deals with the necessity of discipline to bring about Christian conduct and character in individuals' lives.

The church in Corinth was a powerful church, established by Paul himself. He was writing to them to deal with some of the excesses and difficulties that they were facing with the hope of bringing correction to the problems there. He first brought a picture of his own apostolic authority and ability to speak to the needs and the problems of the time. His focus was to bring cleansing to the church of false conceptions of the ministry, pride, and social evils.

This is a very practical book, which covers a wide variety of subjects, which are still germane today. Even though germane, we must recognize the need to understand his writings within cultural context. Not all that is written can be directly applied to our individual life.

As you will see in the outline of this book, the divisions within the church are addressed and the disorders within the church challenged. Paul also answers various questions that must have been posed to him prior to actually writing this letter back to the church. In the second half of the book, we see him deal with the regulations for corporate worship and various teachings on the resurrection of Christ and its importance in our life.

The Apostle Paul, in much of his writings, could be characterized as very doctrinally oriented. But in this book, he primarily deals with the practices of living a Christian life according to the plan of God. God's intention is for all to be men and women of integrity, walking upright with one another. In so doing, he is laying a strong foundation for the believers in the church in Corinth. We can learn much from Paul's writings in this book.

Discipline

1. This book was written to the saints at Corinth but intended for all men. The founding of the church there is described in Acts 18. Paul came to this city on his second missionary journey, late in the year 52 AD. The church at Corinth was composed mainly of Gentiles.

2. The occasion for the epistle was the distressing problems within the church. This epistle is, therefore, essentially one of discipline and correction. There were five specific and serious problems: (a) division among the brethren; (b) condoning of immorality; (c) their lawsuits against one another; (d) their abuse of the Lord's Supper; (e) general disorder in their corporate worship.

These problems within the Corinthian church were due to three kinds of selfishness, which had blinded them spiritually: self-admiration, their intellect had deceived them; self-will, their conscience had been dulled; and self-indulgence, their passions had not been restrained. The greatest danger of the Corinthian church was not from without but from within.

3. Paul's purpose in writing this letter was twofold: to correct the disorders which had arisen within the Corinthian church, and to answer the questions which had been submitted to him.

4. The name "Lord" is very prominent in this epistle (1:31; 2:8, 16; 3:20; 4:4; 5:4; 6:13. etc.) This is very significant, since the trouble within the church was due to their failure to recognize Jesus Christ as Lord. Only as they crown Christ Lord of their lives, will He bring order out of disorder.

5. First Corinthians is intensely practical. It touches upon certain issues in depth more than other books, such as those of Christian liberty, marriage and divorce, the Lord's Supper, the charismatic gifts of the Holy Spirit, women ministries, the meaning of Christian love, the order for corporate worship, and the resurrection from the dead.

6. Relationship of the epistle to surrounding books:
Romans: doctrinal, preparation, establishes foundations, set the norm.
Corinthians: discipline, wrong practice, exposes faults, shows sub-norm.
Galatians: correction, wrong doctrine, shows ab-norm.

Outline
I. Discipline of Christian Conduct (Chs. 1-11)
    A. Division within the Church (1:1-4:21)
    B. Disorders within the Church (5:1-6:20)
    C. Answers to Inquiries (7:1-10:33)
II. Instructions in Christian Conduct (Chs. 12-16)
    A. Regulations for Corporate Worship (11:1-14:40)
    B. Teaching on the Resurrection (15:1-58)

THIRTEEN

2 CORINTHIANS

Consolar

Introduction

The Book of 2 Corinthians is a letter of comfort to the church and is a sequel to 1 Corinthians.

In this letter, the Apostle Paul is writing for the purpose of laying the foundation in preparation to his actual coming to that church. He writes from the heart of a pastor, comforting the people with the same comfort that he had been comforted by God. The Apostle Paul had experienced great difficulties in his life and ministry in terms of the opposition of the devil and devilish people that he encountered. He is saying in the midst of all that, God is able to comfort people with His grace, mercy, love, and kindness.

Throughout this book you will see Paul talking about his ministry and his right to speak into their lives. It is interesting to note that many people who consider themselves spiritual gurus will attempt to speak into the lives of the saints of God without earning that right and respect. The Apostle Paul had the right to speak into the lives of these believers because he had paid the price to do so. He had sacrificed his life on behalf of the sheep, therefore he deserved that double portion of honor.

Another important theme in this book is the need for Christian stewardship, of caring for the needs of others, especially the poor. The greatest theme found in this book is God's ability to comfort and also our responsibility as Christians to give comfort to one another.

81

Comfort

1. This epistle was written to the same circle of readers in the Corinthian church as mentioned in the first epistle.

2. The purpose of this epistle is stated by Paul himself in 13:10. It is to lay the preparatory groundwork necessary before his arrival in order to render him recognized in authority so as to minister edification to them. While the first epistle is essentially disciplinary and corrective, this epistle proposes to build up the body. However, Paul must first vindicate his apostolic authority. The Judaistic party there had attacked his apostleship upon the following grounds: (a) they accused Paul of lightness and indecision, purposing at one time to come and then changing his mind (1:16-18); (b) they charged him with pride (1:24); (c) they suggested that he was deceitfully cunning in conduct (12:16); (d) they bluntly denied his apostleship and authority (12:11-12); (e) they attacked his personal appearance as inconsistent with his bold manner of speech. Therefore, most of this epistle attempts to establish Paul's apostolic character and authority.

3. Paul relates more personal history in this epistle than in any other of his letters. He is very concerned with the question of his glorying or boasting, presumably because the Judaistic opposition had raised the question (mentioned 31 times). Personal history related only in this letter: his escape from Damascus in a basket (11:32-33); his being caught up to the third heaven (12:1-4); his thorn in the flesh (12:7); and his suffering (11:23-27).

4. The theme of the book is "comfort." The reason for declaring comfort to the brethren is the all sufficiency of Christ through the bestowal of His grace.
   A. The epistle begins with comfort, "the God of all comfort" (1:3)
   B. The middle of the epistle gives the grounds for their comfort:
      (1) Reason for comfort, "having all sufficiency in all things" (9:8)
      (2) Source of this comfort, "My grace is sufficient" (12:9)
   C. The epistle ends with comfort, "be of good comfort" (13:11)

5. Besides the question of apostleship, the letter treats extensively the subject of liberal giving in chapters 8 and 9. Paul teaches: give even out of poverty (8:2); give generously (8:3); give willingly (8:3); give proportionately (8:12-14); give cheerfully (9:7).

Outline
I. Paul's Ministry (Chs. 1-7)
II. Christian Stewardship (Chs. 8-9)
III. Paul's Apostleship (Chs. 10-13)

FOURTEEN

GALATIANS

Introduction

The letter to the church in Galatia was written by the Apostle Paul. It is not written to one specific church, but to the various churches in the area of Galatia in Asia Minor.

In this book the Apostle Paul is attacking the Judaizers who were teaching that one had to become circumcised and follow the Law and the feasts in order to be a good Christian. It is really one of the finest books you will ever find dealing with the contrast between legalism and liberty. In some ways this book is known as the Declaration of Independence, not independence from God, but independence from legalistic church activity. It is a book whereby encouragement is given to walk in Christian liberty, which is the fulfillment of the law of love.

In this book you'll see the contrast between law and grace, of faith and works, of the flesh and the fruit of Holy Spirit, and the contrast between the world and the cross. Here depicted by the Apostle Paul is the beauty of the cross being activated in one's own life. When we identify with the cross of Christ and allow the cross of Christ to be a focal point of our own lives, the Holy Spirit begins to transform us into the very image of Christ. We recognize that the liberty that Christ has brought us to does not give us permission to sin, but frees us to live a life that is pleasing to God.

Christian Liberty

1. This epistle was written to the churches of Galatia, an area of Asia Minor. There are two theories as to which churches these may be. The North Galatian theory asserts that the churches of Galatia were in the area visited during Paul's second missionary journey (Acts 16:6). However, the South Galatian theory is more acceptable, suggesting that these churches were those of Iconium, Lystra, and Derbe, visited during Paul's first missionary journey (Acts 14) and revisited on the second journey (Acts 16:1-5).

2. The occasion of this epistle is not only the presence of the Judaizing teachers, but also the measure of success they had attained in perverting the Galatian churches. They taught that one had to become a Jewish proselyte and be under the law to be saved. Paul attempts to reassert Christian liberty on the grounds of justification through faith. The letter shows that the believer is no longer under the law but is saved by faith alone.

3. The theme of this epistle is clearly that of Christian liberty. The key verse is Galatians 5:1. This letter has been called the Christian's Declaration of Independence. This "liberty" is not shown to be freedom from law. Rather, liberty is freedom in law. The basis of this liberty is its being "in Christ" (2:4).

4. Galatians is a book of contrasts:
   A. The Contrast of Law and Grace
      1. Law shows us our need; grace shows God's provision for meeting that need.
      2. Law is of works, saying "do;" grace is a free gift, saying "done."
   B. The Contrast of Faith and Works
      1. Faith receives salvation by simply believing.
      2. Works receives salvation by striving to earn it.
   C. The Contrast of the Works of the Flesh and the Fruit of the Spirit
      1. The flesh naturally would produce these works.

2. The fruit of the Spirit must be cultivated and grown to live in victory.
   D. The Contrast of the World and the Cross
   1. The worldly system is based upon selfishness.
   2. The cross system is based upon sacrifice.

5. The comparison of Galatians to the Book of Romans: in Romans we find our standing; in Galatians we take our stand. Both books deal extensively with the subject of justification by faith. However, in Romans Paul treats the subject systematically, while in Galatians he treats it polemically (defending it against error).

Outline

I. Paul Defends His Apostolic Authority: Personal (Chs. 1-2)
II. Paul Defends the Gospel: Doctrinal (Chs. 3-4)
III. Paul Defends the Spirit-led Life: Practical (Chs. 5-6)

FIFTEEN

EPHESIANS

Introduction

In the Book of Ephesians, Paul is writing to the church in Ephesus. The church in Ephesus was a very powerful and solid work that was planted by Paul himself. There were many converted Jews in the early churches who wanted to isolate themselves from Gentile believers. The Apostle Paul saw that as anathema and wrote to express the wonderful unity of the church and how we have all been brought together into a unity of the faith.

Throughout his book we see him describing the revelation of the mystery. From the very beginning of time, from the foundation of the world, the Godhead had determined that the church would be birthed. The church is not an afterthought of God but is His divine plan for the propagation of the gospel of Jesus Christ to the world.

This book reveals the divine origin of the church, the full plan of the salvation of God, the practical application of such a great mysterious and divine plan of God for all mankind. Practically, Paul speaks of a need for unity, the importance of a consistent walk with the Lord Jesus Christ, of dealing with our old nature, renewing our mind and putting on the new self, and walking in the liberty that God has given. He also provides practical teaching in the area of walking in purity and light in our home life, and finally the need for preparation for spiritual warfare.

This is one of the most powerful books written. It has been called the Gospel of the Apostle Paul to the church. A clear and comprehensive picture of the life of God in the believer and the role of the church is powerfully portrayed.

The Body of Christ
1. This epistle was written as an encyclical letter (intended for general circulation). Thus it is devoid of the customary personal salutations of the Apostle Paul.

2. Paul's purpose in this letter was not so much to combat error as to further establish the truth. He desired to strengthen their faith and encourage their hopes. Paul's approach is in summing up all things in Christ, that is, the things in the heavens and the things upon the earth (1:9-10). The major emphasis is on the body of Christ, the church, which is ordained of God to carry out this program.

3. The theme of the book is the unraveling of the mystery of the body of Christ. The "mystery" is that the Gentiles are to have an equal position with the Jews (3:6). The church is not an organization but an organism, the body of Christ, of which Christ is the head. Every believer is a member of Christ's body.

4. Both Ephesians and Colossians emphasize the truth of the church as the body of which Christ is the Head. Colossians sets forth the dignity of Christ, with emphasis upon His Headship, while Ephesians sets forth the sublimity of the church, with emphasis upon the nature of the body. Also, as to style, Colossians is largely controversial, while Ephesians is almost free from controversial elements.

5. The content of Ephesians may be viewed with reference to three different postures of the believer:
    A. Sitting (Chapters 1-2): The believer's position is described as being seated with Christ in the heavenlies (2:6).

90

B. Walking (Chapters 3-4): The believer is called on to walk in a manner fitting his calling (4:1).

C. Standing (Chapters 5-6): The believer's life is seen as a warfare in which he must stand against the wiles of the devil (6:11).

6. The first half of the book (chapters 1-3) elaborately describes what are the blessings of the believer who is in Christ: blessed in Christ (1:3), chosen in Him (1:4), adopted by Christ (1:5), accepted in the beloved (1:6), forgiven in Christ (1:7), all things centered in Christ (1:10), an inheritance in Christ (1:11), glorified in Christ (1:12-13), have faith in Christ (1:15), wisdom in Him (1:17), hope in Christ (1:18), power in Christ (1:19-20), quickened in Christ (2:5-6), created in Christ (2:10), made nigh in Christ (2:13), growing in Christ (2:21), built in Christ (2:22), and boldness through Christ (3:12).

Outline
I. The Believer's Position (Chs. 1-3)
II. The Believer's Conduct (Chs. 4-6)

Salvation is Free
Faith needs to grow

Rejoice in Midst of Difficulty

SIXTEEN

PHILIPPIANS

Introduction

The letter to the Philippians, written to the church in Philipi and to be distributed to other churches, addresses the need for the church to rejoice even in the midst of difficulty. This is a book of joy and rejoicing with the central theme being the Lord Jesus Christ Himself.

In this book we see Jesus as the source of our spiritual life. He's the reason that we preach and proclaim the Word. He is the highest motivation for every Christian to serve God with gladness of heart. He is the only perfect One and our example for living. He is the totality of knowledge and our supreme prize that we are to seek after.

When we consider His coming, we rejoice with great joy. He has unlimited power and the ability to bring about divine supply, exceedingly, abundantly above all that we ask or can even think. Christ will supply. We see it as a beautiful picture of the joy and zest for living in that intimate relationship with our Lord and Savior Jesus Christ.

Rejoice

1. This epistle is written to the church at Philipi, the first church which Paul founded in Europe. The founding of the church is described in Acts 16. Paul had come there in response to a vision and the Macedonian call (Acts 16:9).

2. The purpose of this epistle was primarily to express his gratitude for a gift which the Philippians had sent to him, and also to send them a fervent admonition to steadfastness and humility.

3. This epistle distinguishes itself as a letter of commendation, having no notes of condemnation in it. In this manner it is markedly in contrast with Galatians. It is a letter of thanksgiving to God, love for the converts at Philipi, and joy at their spiritual welfare.

4. A peculiar feature of this book is its general absence of doctrinal discussions. The epistle is more concerned with practice than with doctrine. The only exception perhaps is the reference to Christ's humiliation and exaltation (2:5-11), which comes the closest to Paul's affirmation of Christ's deity.

5. This epistle describes the joyous Christian life. Paul's joy comes not from his circumstances (he was then a prisoner), but from the Lord Himself as source. The word *joy* or *rejoice* occurs sixteen times in the book. Here Paul is the rejoicing apostle. The key verse is 3:1.

6. Christ is beautifully portrayed throughout this epistle in relation to His body. Paul mentions the Savior's name forty times in this short epistle. In reference to His body, He is presented in the following manner: Christ, the believer's life (ch. 1); Christ, the believer's example (ch. 2); Christ, the believer's hope (ch. 3); Christ, the believer's strength (ch. 4).

Outline

I. Joy in Living (Ch. 1)
II. Joy in Service (Ch. 2)
III. Joy in Fellowship (Ch. 3)
IV. Joy in Rewards (Ch. 4)

Happiness is emotional caused by external.
Joy is a fruit of the Spirit
Joy is an attitude

The epistle closes with a final exhortation to remain true, for life could bring no problem which could not be overcome with the help of Christ (Phil. 4:8-13).

94

SEVENTEEN

COLOSSIANS

Sufficiency of Christ

Introduction

The Book of Colossians, as you will see in your outline, deals with the all sufficiency of our Lord and Savior Jesus Christ.

This epistle was written to reinforce the concept that is presented in the Book of Acts: in Him (Jesus) we live, and move, and have our being. It was written to the church in Colossae, which is a city in the area of Asia Minor. It was a very powerful church thought to have been founded by Epaphras.

The Apostle Paul confronts doctrinal error to ensure that no philosophy of men or humanistic ideology will influence their walk with God. In the book you will see the laying of the foundation for the Lordship of Christ. Paul had great concern about that local church. He also deals doctrinally with the supremacy, transcendence, and glory of Christ. His power, demonstrated by His death and resurrection liberates us from the old life. He gives warning regarding worship of anything other than Christ and against becoming overly religious in daily activities.

As is characteristic of most of Paul's writings, he deals with some very practical issues as well. This includes family life and how we are to operate within a local fellowship. The need for us to be constantly in prayer for one another and to remember to give and nurture the poor as Christ would have, is presented as a duty for all believers as an outgrowth of God's marvelous grace imputed to us.

95

The All-Sufficiency of Christ

1. This epistle was written to a church which Paul had not yet visited (1:4, 7, 8; 2:1). The epistle implies that Epaphras had founded the Colossian church (1:7). Philemon's house provided a meeting place for the church. Archippus, mentioned in 4:17, was probably the resident pastor of this church.

2. The purpose of this epistle was to combat heresies of Jewish Gnosticism, which had made inroads in the church at Colossae. The two chief heretical views Paul fights are: according to the Gnostics, there were in the universe many beings of varying degrees, ranging from man to God, Christ was viewed as a superior being but not as God; and there was proposed a false asceticism.

3. Paul's approach is not an indignant attack but rather to make an effective presentation of counter-truths. Here Paul carefully sets forth the supremacy of Christ above all principalities and powers (1:13-19) and the completeness of His redemption (1:20-21). He also shows that true spirituality is not asceticism but a positive new life in Christ, producing purity of thought and conduct.

4. This epistle has a special Christological character. It deals specifically with the person and work of Christ. It emphasizes Christ as to His Headship to His body. It serves to establish the majesty and glory of Christ.

5. The book is divided into two major sections. The first half of the letter (chs. 1-2) pertains to doctrine, while the second half deals with practical considerations. The practical portion is in many respects like a condensation of Ephesians. The doctrinal section sets forth the supremacy and sufficiency of Christ; the practical section sets forth a contrast of the old man (3:9) and the new man (3:10) in Christ.

6. Further admonitions to the Colossians include those against philosophy, legalism, ritualism, enticing words, and angel worship (2:4-21). They

are to "hold the Head" (2:19), which means to have a true understanding of the glories of Christ.

Outline
I. The Head of the Body of Christ (Chs. 1-2)
II. The Life of the Body of Christ (Chs. 3-4)

The epistle ends with a mention of the rich collection of fellow-workers in the gospel with whom Paul had fellowship. Note the distinguishing peculiarities of each one.

EIGHTEEN

1 THESSALONIANS

Introduction

The letter of 1 Thessalonians was written by the Apostle Paul and is probably the earliest of Paul's letters.

The church in Thessalonica was founded by the Apostle Paul on his second missionary journey. He received tremendous opposition to the planting of the church and ministry to the Greeks. Yet the power of the Holy Spirit was evident to bring about salvation in this community of Greek believers.

The primary themes of this book include commendations, personal reminiscences and counsel, and exhortation on living the Christian life. Again, it is a very practical book that deals with issues of hope as one anticipates the Second Coming of the Lord Jesus Christ.

In this book we see the Apostle Paul giving great commendation to those that walk faithfully before the Lord. In view of the fact that Christ is coming again, we need to live a life of faithfulness before Him and to live out our life and fulfill our obligations until He comes. In light of that, we need to live a life of purity since we do not know when He might return.

Further, we are to live in hope, recognizing that at the Second Coming of Christ, we will see again those who have gone on to be with the Lord. We need to remain watchful in light of the fact that Christ is coming. It is our blessed hope that we have as Christians. No specific time frame is given by Paul predicting the coming of Christ. It is apparent throughout his writings that they had a sense He could come back in their time. It is interesting that every church age has had the same sense. Certainly Christ must come in our time! We hope as believers that Christ will come during our generation, but until that time, we must occupy, work, and labor for the sake of the kingdom, until He comes.

The Coming of the Lord
1. This epistle is written to the church at Thessalonica, which was planted by Paul in the course of his second missionary journey (Acts 17:1-10). Although Paul was evidently there only one month, the church was firmly established through Paul's teaching ministry.

2. This book is the first epistle written by the Apostle Paul. The purpose of this writing is to correct some misunderstandings that the Thessalonians had regarding the return of Christ. Their misconceptions were basically two: they were in sorrow concerning some who had died, having become believers, thinking that these would have no part in Christ's second coming; and their concept of the imminence of the Lord's return had caused them to cease their work and sit idly waiting for the return (4:11-18). *Rapture of the Church*

3. Paul's answers to these erroneous concepts were these, that the hope of the deceased believer was based on faith in Christ's death and resurrection. The believing dead will be resurrected and be the first to meet the Lord at His coming (4:13-18). And Paul instructed them to go to work, attend to their own business as usual, and not sit around and wait (4:11-12).

4. The major subject of this epistle is obviously the Lord's return, mentioned in every chapter of the book (1:10; 2:19; 3:13; 4:13-18; 5:23). Paul states that the Second Coming was to serve for comfort and encouragement, but not as an excuse for idleness or speculation about unknown times. The coming of the Lord is accompanied throughout the Scriptures by commands for living godly, and so they are told to "watch

and be sober" (5:6). The Second Coming of Christ is mentioned 318 times in the 260 chapters of the New Testament (a ratio of once every twenty verses).

5. The theme of the epistle is in regards to the believer's walk in view of the coming of the Lord. The believer is to "walk worthy of God" (2:12; 3:13; 4:1, 7, 12; 5:23). The content of the book strives, therefore, for the securing of purity of life and industry of service, more than just instruction in doctrine.

6. The frequent use of the name "Lord" for Jesus is distinguishing here. The title is used twenty-five times in the book. Being Paul's first letter, it was important to establish the Lordship of Christ. Furthermore, the Lordship of Christ is clearly to be tied to the glorification due Him at His Second Coming, and thus is frequently mentioned here.

Outline
I. Faithfulness in View of Christ's Coming (Ch. 1)
II. Service in View of Christ's Coming (Ch. 2)
III. Purity in View of Christ's Coming (Ch. 3)
IV. Comfort in View of Christ's Coming (Ch. 4)
V. Watchfulness in View of Christ's Coming (Ch. 5)

Rapture - Church will be taken
2nd coming -

Triumph in Tribulation Apostasy

NINETEEN

2 Thessalonians

Introduction

Shortly after Paul wrote the first letter to the church in Thessalonica, he wrote a second one. In this writing he deals with some of the misunderstandings that must have occurred because of the first letter. He clarifies things concerning the Second Coming of Christ.

The Apostle Paul corrects the misunderstanding that many had that the Second Coming of Christ was imminent and guaranteed in their lifetime. He helped them to understand that the timing of the man of lawlessness or the man of sin, the man of eminent wickedness, would come before the Second Coming of Christ. He does not give any clear indication through his writings of when that actual time would be. He does lay out even as Christ did in Matthew 25, some of the general signs of the times that would come. Unrest would come and various events would occur, including apostasy in the church, the self-exaltation of the man of sin, even that a satanic personage would arise that would ultimately be destroyed at the coming of Christ. He gives an appeal to all Christians to live according to sound doctrine.

In this letter we also see how the Apostle Paul, in a very vulnerable manner, shares that we must live life in positive response to one another. We are to patiently endure with each other, not to allow busybodies and idle talk to go on, but to respect one another, and labor with one another for the sake of the kingdom of God.

Triumph in Tribulation

1. The second epistle to the church at Thessalonica was probably written from Corinth soon after 1 Thessalonians. A report of the status of affairs at Thessalonica since the reception of the first epistle had come to Paul.

2. This second epistle serves to correct misunderstandings concerning the "Day of the Lord." False teachers had led them to believe that the great and dreadful "Day of the Lord" had already come. The believers at Thessalonica were suffering persecution, which further distressed them with the thought that they were passing through the Tribulation (1:4-7).

3. Paul shows that two specific events must take place before the "Day of the Lord" will be ushered in: a great apostasy must set in, a falling away from the faith; and the revealing of the "man of lawlessness" or the "man of sin" will take place. This term of the coming Antichrist is a Hebraism, meaning "man of eminent wickedness." The sin of man has its final fruition in the Man of Sin (2:1-12).

4. The tone of this epistle is more severe and official than the previous epistle. Here he must give more stern warnings, including those against spurious epistles. Some forged letters and false verbal messages purported to be from him had helped to deceive the Thessalonicans.

5. Paul takes this opportunity to encourage them in their tribulation, especially to patience and trustfulness (1:4). He assures them that there will be a time of righteous judgments when wrongs are righted and vengeance will be meted out to all the oppressors (1:5-7). They are furthermore to take the delay of the Lord's coming for opportunities of service for Him. These opportunities he discusses in 3:1-15.

Outline
I. Tribulation and the Lord's Coming (1:1-7)
II. The Unconverted and the Lord's Coming (1:7-12)
III. The Signs before the Lord's Coming (2:1-12)
IV. Service and the Lord's Coming (2:13-3:18)

TWENTY

1 TIMOTHY

Introduction

There are several examples of father/son relationships within the Word of God. The most supreme, of course, being that of Jesus and His Father. We have also seen in the patriarchs how the father endeavored to pass on to the son that which was required for successful living.

In the Book of 1 Timothy, and also in 2 Timothy, we see how the Apostle Paul is writing to give counsel and exhortation to his son in the Lord, who was a young pastor at the church in Ephesus. In it he deals with the need for Timothy to stay true to the doctrine that Paul had taught him, to be aware of those that would try to undermine the church through legalistic teaching. He was encouraging Timothy, as a young man, to fulfill the vision and the calling that God had placed upon his life.

A sense of Paul's heart, in terms of his love for Timothy, can be found in this book. He wanted Timothy to counteract the development of heresy and to raise up faithful men and faithful women who would be able to continue the ministry. He focused on the qualifications of bishops and deacons in terms of their spiritual maturity in a similar way that Jethro did with Moses as father-in-law to son-in-law. He further counselled Timothy in terms of his ministry of teaching and caring for the sheep.

In the fifth and sixth chapters, we see the Apostle Paul dealing again with very practical matters concerning the old and the young, concerning widows, church elders and their duties, regarding the duties of servants, of how to deal with contentions in the church. He focuses on the peril of riches and the importance of duty in fighting the good fight of the faith. He gives a charge to him to continue on, faithfully fulfilling the call that God has placed upon his life.

It is a beautiful picture of a protective, almost doting father who desperately loves and cares for his son Timothy, hoping to provide to him tools for successful ministry. What a wonderful model for ministry training in the body of Christ today.

Spiritual Overight

1. This letter was written to Timothy, a native of Lystra, whose mother was a Jewess and whose father was a Greek. He was converted through Paul at the age of fifteen years on Paul's first missionary journey (Acts 16:1). Seven years afterwards he became Paul's companion.

2. This epistle was occasioned by the fact that Paul had been suddenly called to Macedonia where he would be delayed. Timothy had been left in charge of the Ephesian church (1:3). This epistle was written to instruct Timothy concerning problems which he would face as a spiritual leader in the church.

3. The purpose of the epistle then was twofold: to exhort Timothy to counteract the development of heresies of the time (Timothy seems to have been timid and retiring by temperament, see 2 Timothy 1:6-8); and to instruct him in the particulars of his duties as overseer and the function of others in the Ephesian church.

4. The theme of this epistle seems to be "behavior in the household of God" (3:15). In this regard, instructions are given concerning prayer and worship; the behavior that qualifies a man for spiritual leadership (chs. 2-3). In chapters 4-6 instructions are given concerning spiritual duties.

5. The earlier epistles laid the doctrinal foundation for the church. This epistle lays down the governmental foundation for the church. The

qualifications for these offices are set forth in 3:1-13. Practical advice is given in chapters 4-6 for governing the flock of God: they are to avoid all kinds of heresies and watch their own conduct (4:1-10), they must give time to study (4:11-16), and they must exercise discretionary caution in dealing with various groups within the church (5:1-6, 10).

6. Paul emphasizes in this letter not so much the teaching of sound doctrine but rather the reasons for the imperative need of sound doctrine. He shows that the real end of all doctrine is love (1:5). This essentially differentiated sound doctrine from false doctrine.

Outline
I. The Need of Sound Doctrine (Ch. 1)
II. The Nature of Prayer (2:1-8)
III. The Necessary Qualifications for Spiritual Oversight (2:9-3:16)
IV. The Nurturing of Spiritual Duties (Chs. 4-6)

TWENTY-ONE

2 TIMOTHY

Loyalty

Introduction

In the second letter to Timothy, we see the Apostle Paul continuing to instruct him as a young pastor in his ministerial duties. He also has a special request to Timothy. Paul had a need that he could freely ask of his son as a spiritual father. The request would have been considered virtually a command to young Timothy to bring to Paul things that he would need for his comfort.

This letter is very personal from Paul's heart. He is trying to strengthen Timothy, who apparently was rather timid and possibly a frail young man. He is urging him not to be ashamed of his testimony and of presenting the gospel of Jesus Christ to those to whom he was called to preach.

In the book we see his great love for his son and his desire to see him become a strong spiritual soldier. He likens that to an athlete and a husbandman. As a spiritual athlete, he must keep the rules of the game; as a husbandman of a vineyard, he needs to expect fruit. He wants him to keep in mind truths that have been taught to him by the Apostle Paul. He further counsels him against heresies and those that would try and bring legalism upon the church and assists him in dealing with things of strife and other difficulties that might arise.

Paul also addresses the apostasy and social corruption that he believed would come and Timothy's need to fight against these through the power of prayer and the ministry of the Word.

In the last section of the letter, Paul gives a solemn charge to Timothy. Again, he encourages him, exhorting him to be faithful. Since Paul was at the end of his road, I believe he wanted, more than anything else, to pass on every bit of advice that he could to young Timothy. He notes the companionship, the love that he has, how much of a comfort Timothy has been to him. He urges him to come for a visit because the Apostle Paul knew that he may not be long for this world. He wanted so desperately to see his son one last time.

There is such a need in these days for that father/son relationship within the body of Christ. The older men are to teach the younger men, the older women are to teach the younger women, passing on a rich spiritual heritage one to another. This will ensure the development and the furtherance of the gospel, which is the responsibility of the mature in Christ.

Loyalty

1. Written also to Timothy, this epistle was the last letter written by Paul just before his martyrdom. He was a prisoner at Rome, closely confined within a dungeon. He expected soon to be executed (4:6), and so he was on some day in May, 68 AD. According to tradition, the Apostle was led outside of Rome on the Ostian road and accorded the death of a Roman citizen, that of beheading.

2. The threefold Roman accusations against the Christians, which rendered their persecution so intense, were: they were accused of atheism, since they denied the Roman gods; they were accused of hatred of the human race, since they lived separated and different from the wickedness of other peoples; and they were accused of being lawbreakers, since they continued to serve and worship God when they were forbidden.

3. The purpose and theme of the letter unite under the metaphor of "a good soldier of Jesus Christ" (2:3). The conduct of this soldier is

essentially to be one of loyalty under any circumstance. This loyal soldier is further to evidence conduct as exemplary (ch. 1), courageous (ch. 2), steadfast (ch. 3), and fervent (ch. 4).

4. This epistle joins with the Books of 2 Peter and Jude to warn of apostasy which had already begun to be evidenced. The voices of such apostasy are clearly enumerated in 3:1-9.

5. This epistle is rich in its metaphors. Timothy is exhorted to be: a courageous soldier (2:1-4; 4:7-8), a careful athlete (2:5; 4:7-8), a faithful farmer (2:6), a diligent workman (2:15), a clean vessel (2:20-21), a gentle servant of the Lord (2:24-26), and a trusted steward or trustee (4:8).

6. Paul, himself facing perilous times, instructs Timothy in the secret of remaining loyal in distressing times. He instructs him that Timothy's knowledge of the Word of God is what will sustain him in loyalty to God and others (3:14-17).

7. Timothy is warned against three things which can cause him to become disloyal as a "good soldier." They are: love of self (3:2), love of pleasure (3:4), and love of the world (4:10).

Outline
I. Loyalty to the Lord in Spite of Suffering (Ch. 1)
II. Loyalty to the Lord in Christian Service (Ch. 2)
III. Loyalty to the Lord in Spite of Apostasy (3:1-5)
IV. Loyalty to the Lord in Spite of Desertion of Others (4:6-22)

TWENTY-TWO

Piedad

TITUS

Introduction

The letter to Titus was written by the Apostle Paul. Titus was a Gentile and beloved friend and helper of Paul. He was a messenger to the church at Corinth, and was a very trustworthy and unselfish man who was a companion of Paul and Barnabus on their journey to Jerusalem.

Apparently Paul had left Titus in Crete as the overseer of various churches. And he was in Rome with Paul during Paul's later imprisonment. He seems to have been more of a sturdy man than Timothy and perhaps more mature. The Apostle Paul is writing to encourage him to go on to even further godliness.

Though there is a lack of doctrinal teaching in the Book of Titus, there is an emphasis on purity of doctrine for good living. He also focuses on the ministerial duties of Titus as an overseer or bishop of the various churches in his area. As such, he encourages him to bring the church in proper order and discipline since the Spirit of God will flow through proper order. He also encourages him to present sound doctrine, to respect those that are elderly, to teach and exhort young men and young women, and to live a life of godliness. This is especially important when you recognize that this is a church that did not have the foundation of spiritual teaching as the Hebrews would have. It expresses the need for a solid foundation to be built for each believer. The Law and the prophets were not studied for the most part by those that were in the Greek and Roman churches.

Therefore, there remained the tremendous need to lay that strong foundation. Paul also urges Titus to fight the heresies, especially the Gnostic teachings and Jewish legalism, and finally expresses the blessed hope that we have because we are saved by the grace and the mercy of God.

Godliness

1. This letter is written to Titus, one of Paul's converts (1:4). Titus had accompanied Paul and Barnabas to Jerusalem at the conclusion of their first missionary journey (Galatians 2:1). Titus was a pure Gentile and was not circumcised (Galatians 2:3).

2. Three things seem to have occasioned the writing of this epistle: the condition of the work in Crete (Titus had been given the responsibility of ministering to the church on the island of Crete, see 1:5), Titus' need of instruction and encouragement, and the going of Zenas and Apollos to the island.

3. Paul's purpose here is much like that in 1 Timothy and the books bear a similar objective: to relate God's ideal for a local church, namely orderly organization in government, soundness in faith, and practical works of ministry; and to relate God's ideal for a Christian worker, namely godliness of life, sound faith, a sober disposition, and chastened speech.

4. The theme of the book is the essentiality of godly conduct by all who are believers. The key phrase of this epistle is "good works" (2:7, 14; 3:8, 14; cf. 1:16; 3:1, 5). The key passage in the book is 2:11-14.

5. Here Titus is charged to oppose false teachers. The heresies assailed in this epistle were of Jewish and not Gnostic origin. Many Jews resided on the island.

6. The Cretans are not given a good character reference by Paul. He quotes the words of one of their own poets and asserts that this testimony was true: "The Cretans are always liars, evil beasts, slow bellies" (1:12). They were noted as being a turbulent race, neither peaceable among themselves nor very patient of foreigners. Thus Paul knew that the charges concerning church order were vitally important and would be undoubtedly unwelcome, even by most of the Cretan converts. Paul had entrusted Titus to a delicate mission.

7. Because of the turbulent temperament of the Cretans, Paul finished his epistle with giving a specific method of dealing with heretics and problem people (3:9-11). They are to be rebuked sharply and rejected if not brought to repentance after two admonitions. These guidelines are obviously still to be followed today, for they are timeless and true.

Outline
I. Instruction on an Orderly Church (Ch. 1)
II. Instruction on a Sound Church (Ch. 2)
III. Instruction on a Practical Church (Ch. 3)

TWENTY-THREE

PHILEMON

Introduction

The short letter from the Apostle Paul to Philemon, a resident of Colosse, is a rather private letter of intercession from Paul on behalf of Onesimus. Onesimus was a runaway slave of Philemon, and in this letter the Apostle Paul is pleading his case to Philemon to receive back Onesimus. Though a runaway, he had become a devoted disciple of Christ and a very close and masterful helper for the Apostle Paul.

This letter is a most beautiful letter of intercession, pleading for forgiveness and restoration of Onesimus as a personal favor to the Apostle Paul. In the letter Paul reminds Philemon of his duty of Christian brotherhood to restore Onesimus. He was to receive him as though he was receiving Paul himself. The Apostle Paul, of course, had given much of his life to Philemon and to the church and had every right to ask a favor, which was really not a favor. He must receive him because it is the Word from the Apostle Paul.

This is a story of restoration, brotherly love, and the duty of obedience to the Word of God on the part of converts. Onesimus needed to return to his master, to complete his restoration. Though a loss to the Apostle, he was more concerned for Onesimus and Philemon's growth and relationship than his own comfort.

Outline
I. Salutation (1-3)
II. Paul's Love for Philemon (4-7)
III. The Appeal for Onesimus (8-16)
IV. Promise of Paul to Philemon (17-22)
V. Greetings and Benediction (23-25)

TWENTY-FOUR

HEBREWS

How to live life to the max in Christ

Introduction

Although the authorship of the Book of Hebrews is not fully known, it is attributed to either Paul, Barnabas, Luke, or perhaps even Apollos. However, most people do favor Paul's authorship.

This letter was written primarily to Hebrew Christians wherever they might be found. In it the writer focuses on the danger of relapsing into Judaism, or at least giving too much credence to ceremonial observances. It's primarily a doctrinal book that also has some practical teaching and exhortation.

In this book we see Christ having brought a better covenant than the old covenant. In the New Testament, Christ had a higher calling, a heavenly calling as our Great High Priest. Because of the work that He has done, we can also rest in the labor that He has completed.

In Hebrews we see the preeminence of Christ presented and of Christ's priesthood and the appeal to us also to be a part of the priesthood of Christ, all of us being individual priests unto Him. He shows how Christ was priest similar to Melchisedec, who was a type of Christ.

In the section on practical teaching, we see believers exhorted to steadfastness and mutual encouragement as the grace of God is worked out in their lives. There are strong warnings against backsliding and of becoming a ceremonial believer rather than going on to follow the teachings and precepts of Christ.

In the famous eleventh chapter, we see the roll call of faith and the heroes both of victory and defeat. We see the need for Christian discipline, to be watchful, and to live a life where Christ is preeminent amongst all things.

It is a very powerful book on living life to its fullest by faith, faith in the preeminence of Christ who brought a more full and complete covenant through His own blood.

Outline
I. Introduction: Christ the Final Revelation (1:1-3)
II. Christ Better Than the Angels (1:4-2:18)
III. Christ Better than Moses and Joshua (3:1-4:13)
IV. Christ Better than the Aaronic Priesthood (4:14-7:28)
V. Christ the Better Covenant (8:1-10:18)
VI. Faith the Better Way (10:19-12:29)
VII. Conclusion (13:1-25)

TWENTY-FIVE

JAMES

Patience *How to live a consecrated life*

Introduction

Although some dispute the authorship of the book, most would agree it is written by James, half-brother of our Lord Jesus Christ. It was apparently written to Jewish converts who lived outside of the holy land. Their departure was caused by the great persecution that came into Jerusalem.

It is a very practical letter dealing with issues of patience and of practical faith lived out in spiritual works. In this book the writer discusses the difference between true and false religion. The marks of a true religion are joy and patience amidst difficulty and unwavering faith, acceptance of one's position in life, and the ability to endure during times of temptation and trial.

James also instructs us in the recognition of the sources of temptation, the results of yielding to them, and the recognition of God's ability and power to give blessing to His children. He also shares the importance of spiritual hearing and of patience when provoked, forsaking of evil and meekness which is quiet strength, and receiving the truth that God has for us. In fact, it indicates the need to search out the truth and to live a life of great purity.

James focuses on the need for good works as a proof of our faith. Mere intellectual assent to the doctrines of Christ will not bring change. Nor will our works bring rewards for the Christian if the works are done for work's sake only. Works, which come out of a believing and saving faith, will bring ultimate rewards for Christians here on earth and in the kingdom to come.

Finally, James also teaches specifically on living a godly life, of warnings for the rich, exhortations in regard to the coming of the Lord, instructions having to do with pastoral life, such as prayer, healing, confession, and the duty to continue to take the gospel of Christ to the world.

Patience

1. The author, James, was "the Lord's brother" (Galatians 1:19), being the son of Joseph and Mary, and thus a half brother of the Lord. In Matthew 13:55, he is mentioned first in a group of four brethren of Christ and was apparently the eldest son of Joseph and Mary.

2. This epistle is one of the most practical books in the New Testament. The writer deals with everyday affairs, covering such matters as one's speech, business ventures, personal relationships with others, disagreements, employment relations, and other problems which continually affect our lives.

3. While Peter discusses the testing of faith, James is concerned with the endurance of "patience" of faith through trials. James approaches faith by applying it to every area of human life. The key verse is 1:4. The word *patience* occurs seven times in the book, distinctively at the beginning and conclusion of the epistle (1:3, 4; 5:7, 8, 10, 11).

4. Patience in James is more than a calm resignation to the inevitable. Verse 1:4 suggests that the patience of James is active. It "works." As various trials come upon us, we are to persevere in patience in order that its perfect work of refining us may be completed in our lives. Patience involves the understanding that we are being "perfected" by God.

5. A sub-theme of James is wisdom. To have working patience, we must have a true wisdom to discern the divine dealings of God and to profit by

them. James has been called "The Epistle of Christian Wisdom," whereas 2 Peter emphasized "knowledge" of God's Word. James, in his practical thrust, emphasizes "wisdom" applied to our lives. This wisdom is described in 3:17. The way to receive this wisdom is simply to "ask" (1:5).

6. James has a remarkable similarity in his epistle to the Sermon on the Mount (Matthew 5-7). It is obvious that this letter is a purposely designed commentary on this great discourse of the Lord. The Bible student will profit greatly by studying the parallels of each one.

7. James strongly emphasizes the necessity of prayer in the everyday life of the believer. James himself was known as a man of prayer. Tradition says that he prayed so much that his knees became hard and callused like a camel's knees. He urges prayer in his closing section of 5:16-18.

Outline
I. The Test of Patience (1:1-27)
II. The Nature of Patience (2:1-3:12)
III. The Words of Patience (3:13-4:17)
IV. The Application of Patience (4:19-5:20)

TWENTY-SIX

1 PETER

Suffering

Introduction

This book was undoubtedly written by Simon Peter, a disciple and an apostle of our Lord Jesus Christ. Peter is a most interesting character within the New Testament. He was a man of great passion, a man of great inconsistency, and yet one who was used mightily of God to bring the gospel throughout Jerusalem and to the Greeks and Romans as well.

He is writing this letter to Christians who are scattered throughout Asia Minor, both Jew and Gentile converts. These are churches that were largely founded by the Apostle Paul and he is giving a message of encouragement, instruction, and admonition.

First of all, I believe Peter's primary purpose was to encourage and strengthen the believers to feed the flock of God. Throughout the letter of 1 Peter, we see the word *suffering* and that Christ has come to give us victory, salvation, a living hope which will not fade away, and divine power which comes to us through faith. We are even to rejoice in the midst of trials in that God will purify His church and individuals, which is a part of His mysterious foreordained plan.

Peter further exhorts believers to be purified, to become holy and separated unto God, not to allow evil desires to be prominent in the heart, but to be the living stones, vibrant. As Christ is the chief cornerstone, we are to be living stones within the body of Christ. Further, he deals with the believer's position and duties which are honorable. We are to follow civil codes and recognize the duties that we have toward one another and the household of faith.

He has specific teaching on wives, husbands, and children and their relationship to one another. He finalizes his teaching on the need to be aware of those that would try to disrupt the flock, the need to follow the elders within the local church and show them great respect, and to live a life of humility before all mankind. Peter had made tremendous strides from the impetuous man with "foot-in-mouth" tendencies. He is an example that with man it is impossible (salvation, restoration), but with God all things are possible.

Suffering

1. This first letter of Peter was written to "the strangers scattered throughout" various provinces of Asia Minor. This epistle was written about 60 AD from "Babylon" (5:13). The question is whether this reference is to ancient Babylon in Mesopotamia or whether Peter is using the term symbolically for the city of Rome. That Peter refers to Rome seems the best interpretation. The fact that Peter was in Rome is testified to by Ignatius, Papias, Clement, Tertullian, and others.

2. The purpose of the epistle is to encourage believers in times of suffering for Christ. The word *suffering* is prominent in the letter, being found ten times in reference to the believer (2:19, 20; 3:14, 17; 4:1, 13, 15, 19; 5:9, 10) and seven times in reference to Christ (1:11; 2:21, 23; 3:18; 4:1, 13; 5:10).

3. This is the epistle of hope in the midst of suffering. Peter is clearly the Apostle of Hope. Peter's answer to suffering is the word *hope*, found in (1:3, 13, 21; 3:5, 15). He shows Christ as our example in suffering. A basis of hope in suffering is that suffering is a means of winning glory. Peter thus actually exalts suffering.

4. Peter develops his subject of suffering by showing that suffering is the will of God (4:19). Therefore, the believer is actually "called" unto suffering (2:21). This suffering proves our faith and the believer should

expect suffering (4:12) and not to be troubled by it (3:14). The believer should patiently endure (2:23; 3:9) and rejoice in suffering (4:13).

5. This epistle has a practical emphasis. All doctrinal statements can be paralleled elsewhere in the New Testament with the one exception of the subject of the fate of the impenitent dead. It contains no speculative interests, no theological discussions of depth. Peter was a man of action, and whatever he came to understand, he immediately put into practice.

6. Consistent with Peter's temperament as a man of action, this short epistle contains a large number of imperatives, the need of command (34 times). Peter thus shows us that living for Christ makes real demands upon the believer.

Outline
I. The Perspective of the Believer in Suffering (1:1-2:10)
II. The Pressures on the Believer in Suffering (2:11-4:6)
III. The Practice of the Believer in Suffering (4:7-5:14)

TWENTY-SEVEN

2 PETER

Introduction

The letter of 2 Peter is quite different from the first. It deals very little with doctrine but is primarily a letter of warning against corrupt teachers and those that would scoff against the church and God's Word. In this letter, we see Peter writing as a shepherd to sheep with grave concern on his heart.

There was a prevalence of false teaching and a general corruption and apostasy in the society. To counteract that, he instructs on the need for positive spiritual life, to follow the precious promises of God, to remember the teaching of the apostles, and to follow them.

The false teachers and doctrines that Peter fought against included heresies that deny the deity of Christ. He brings judgments against them and warnings. He thoroughly condemns sensuality and excesses of lifestyle, of apostasy, and of living a life of sensuality rather than true Christian liberty, which is to live life according to the primary law of love for God and love for one another.

Peter, recognizing as Paul did, that he was coming to the end of his life, was very concerned that believers everywhere continue steadfastly in the doctrine they had been taught. Pure doctrine is still needed today.

Faithfulness is one of the major themes you will find within the Word of God from Abraham all the way through to the Book of Revelation. There is a call to faithfulness as Christians. It is one of the primary ingredients that is necessary for stability in our walk with Christ. It is desperately needed in our day and time for men and women learn to live faithfully before their God and with one another.

There are those that would scoff against the gospel, and there are those that would try and steal from us our great liberty that was won for us by Christ's death on the cross. Therefore, we must fight the good fight of the faith, and be faithful to what Christ has brought us to.

Knowledge of God's Word

1. Peter's second epistle stands in contrast to his first epistle:

1 Peter	*2 Peter*
Pastoral, fatherly, dignified, gentle	Prophetic, denunciatory, severe
Emphasis upon "hope"	Emphasis upon "knowledge"
Concern about suffering	Concern about false teachings
Consolation	Warning

2. The key emphasis in this epistle is "knowledge," occurring twelve times in 1:2, 3, 5, 6, 8, 16, 20; 2:20, 21; 3:3, 17, 18 (sixteen times in Greek). Peter's antidote to false teaching is true spiritual knowledge. The key to combating false teaching is the knowledge of the truth. Peter must have remembered Hosea's lament, "My people are destroyed for lack of knowledge" (4:6). Peter's quoting in his first epistle from Hosea would support this supposition.

3. The key verse is 3:18. Peter desires that they grow in both the "grace and in the knowledge of our Lord and Savior Jesus Christ." Therefore, they must grow in grace as well as knowledge. This knowledge is more than mere academic concepts. It is a knowledge that must be spiritual and express itself in action. The heretical influence that Peter combats was antinomianism ("against the law") which was the Gnostic influence. Its result was an immoral tendency which manifested in sinful living. Peter exhorts his readers to holiness.

4. This epistle is also eschatological in nature. Here again, Peter is the Apostle of Hope. He presents the hope of the Second Coming of Christ. Peter's application is that the believer should conduct himself accordingly in godliness and faithfulness as he looks for the return of the Lord Jesus Christ (3:11, 12).

5. Peter includes a solemn warning in this epistle against sin and sinners. Judgment is a strong undercurrent in this second epistle. In chapter two he refers to various judgments in Old Testament times: the Flood, the overthrow of Sodom and Gomorrah, and the sinning angels. This judgment is applied in reference to those false teachers who lead others astray (ch. 2) and a future judgment upon the world in sin by fire (ch. 3). They who are judged are guilty of willful ignorance, for true "knowledge" is available if one will but accept it.

Outline
I. The Convictions of Faith, Knowledge and the Believer's Walk (Ch. 1)
II. The Contention for the Faith, Knowledge Opposing Heresies (Ch. 2)
III. The Consummation of the Faith, Knowledge and the Second Coming (Ch. 3)

TWENTY-EIGHT

1, 2, & 3 JOHN

Introduction

All three epistles of John can be commented on since they flow together. The Apostle John was called the beloved apostle. He was the disciple that was closest to Jesus Christ while he was living here on Earth.

The epistles of John are written to his beloved children. In the first one we see John exhorting his precious children to live a life at peace with one another as members of the family of God.

The primary word in 1 John is *love*. We are to live a life of love with one another as brothers and sisters in Christ. He also gives a stern warning for those who do not live affectionately or lovingly with one another.

He stresses the importance of knowing Christ and of knowing one another, to recognize that God is life and light and that the conditions of a divine fellowship is to walk in the light, with confession of sins, in acceptance of Christ as our Advocate. Our need for obedience is seen in the test of fellowship, obedience to Christ, obedience to laws of proper conduct in humanity. He warns against loving the world and the fact that antichrist and apostasy will come. He recognizes that truth is what we must abide in.

In the third chapter of 1 John, he discusses the righteous love of God and the need for us to live a life of brotherly love. We are to walk in truth in the divine love that God has given. He finally deals with faith in love and its overcoming power that through the love of Christ we can be overcomers.

In 2 John we see the walk of truth. That is the key word found throughout this book written to the elect lady and her children. In this small book we see how the Apostle John unites divine truth in relationship to believers. It is united in fellowship, to eternally grow within them. Our truth needs to be connected with love, and through loving obedience we bring truth into one another's life.

He also encourages us to avoid worldly error and not to depart from the teachings of Christ. It is very interesting in our day of no moral absolutes and Madison Avenue mentality, that one of the things that has been lost is the scathing search for truth. It is truth in the inner man that sets us free. Jesus said in the Gospel of John, "You shall know the truth and the truth shall set you free." The freedom that we desperately need comes through the knowledge of truth in the Holy Spirit. We know that our Father is a God of truth and He desires desperately that we keep ourselves from deception, which can be brought into the church through false teachers and false doctrine.

In 3 John we see the key word is *hospitality*. This is written to Gaius, who apparently was an evangelist at the time by the Apostle John. We really don't know who Gaius is, but we know that he was one who was worthy of the affection of John, a consistent Christian who walked in the truth and was a man given to hospitality. He was apparently a pillar in the church who was ambitious and somewhat racist in orientation. He tried to overlord the vineyard of God, and is being rebuked by the apostle. In contrast again, we see Demetrius who was a model church man, a man of positive reputation.

The final word that comes from the apostle is a word regarding Christian ministries. Those who preach and teach are worthy of welcome hospitality and honor. Those that are giving the pure milk and meat of the Word are certainly deserving of double honor.

Family Love (1 John)

1. 1 John is closely related to John's Gospel. Whereas John's Gospel asserts Christ's deity, the epistle emphasizes His humanity. The Gospel

gives an announcement of salvation while the epistle gives the assurance of salvation. Thus, the key verse is 5:13. Both speak of Christ as "the Word" and have very similar vocabulary.

2. John is the apostle of love. The word *love* occurs more often in this book than in any other New Testament book. The word and its derivatives occur 51 times in the epistle. Love here is God's very essence and center from which all His attributes spring. This love is to be likewise manifested through believers.

3. John wrote against the Docetic Gnostics who denied the reality of Christ's humanity. This was an oriental dualism taught in Ephesus in John's day which regarded evil as an eternal attribute of matter. Thus flesh was considered evil and Christ, so they reasoned, could not have had a fleshly body to be sinlessly perfect.

4. John deals in this epistle with opposites: death and life, darkness and light, confidence and fear, righteousness and unrighteousness, Christ and antichrist, love of God and love of the world.

5. John emphasizes the concept of the "family" of God. Whereas Paul conceives of the natural man as out of favor with God, John conceives of the natural man as outside of the family of God. The terms in the letter reveal it as a family letter and those who are believers are the "children of God" and in His family (3:1, 2; 5:1, 2).

6. A sub-theme of this epistle is that of fellowship. The word is used by John to describe the ideal relationship between God and His children (1:3, 6, 7). Some have seen "fellowship" as the keynote to the book. Chapter one shows the requirements for fellowship; 2:1-17, the character of fellowship; 2:18-20, the enemies of fellowship; chapter 3, the tests of fellowship; chapter 4, the practice of fellowship; 5:1-12, the foundation of fellowship; 5:13-21, the privileges of fellowship. Fellowship is the practical realization of family love.

Outline
I. The Basis of Family Love (1:5-2:29)
II. The Nature of Family Love (3:1-4: 6)
III. The Results of Family Love (4:5-5:12)

Walking in Truth (2 John)

1. 2 John is a personal note, sent by the Apostle John to an "elect lady and her children" whose names are unknown. It appears from verse 10 that she had entertained itinerant ministry who had visited the community. John had been impressed with their devotion to the truth. This epistle is written, of course, to all believers as well.

2. The key word is *truth*. John knew how persistent the false teachers were in this area. He entreats the lady and others to be "walking in truth" and to keep the Lord's commandments (5-6). He warns her against the deceivers that were abroad.

3. Those who deny truth and the doctrine of Christ are not to be given a Christian greeting (10-11). Truth is seen here as the body of teaching which believers have received from God. All teachers and teachings are to be tested by the truth.

Outline
I. The Truth of the Father (1-6)
II. The Deception of the Deceivers (7-13)

Hospitality (3 John)

1. This is the shortest book in the New Testament (in Greek). It is directed towards one named Gaius of whom nothing else is recorded in Scripture.

2. The key word is *hospitality*. The letter commends the hospitable spirit of Gaius in showing "an open door" policy to believers and strangers (5). He is encouraged to continue his ministry of love.
3. In direct contrast to this was the spirit of Diotrephes. Itinerant ministry, evidently sent by John, had visited the church, but Diotrephes had spoken

against the apostle and had refused to recognize the messengers of the gospel and had opposed those who received them. It seems that he wanted to have the preeminence. The actions and spirit of Diotrephes are severely condemned.

Outline
I. The Commendation of Gaius' Hospitality (1-8)
II. The Condemnation of Diotrephes' Hostility (9-14)

TWENTY-NINE

JUDE

Introduction

This letter was written probably by Jude himself, who focuses on the perils of unbelief. This is a letter of warning. In it we see the warning against immoral teachers and the tremendous amount of heretical teachings, which were being presented, which endangered the very faith of believers that Christ had died for.

The letter was written as a defensive of faith. It warns against punishment that comes for backsliding and likens the punishment of Israel as a type, similar to the fate of fallen angels. The characteristics of depraved teachers are described with great clarity. References to various prophecies are presented and he summarizes Christian duties as mutual edification and prayerfulness, of giving love toward God, trusting Christ for our salvation, and of being active in the local church especially, as it comes to soul winning.

It is a very interesting book. It is a book of faith and warning especially written as for those days but which we can easily speak to our present condition.

Perils of Unbelief

1. The author of this epistle identifies himself as Jude and "brother of James" (1). This would then make him to be a half-brother of the Lord Jesus.

2. This letter is an exhortation "to contend earnestly for the faith" (3), whereas 2 Peter anticipates the problem of false teachers coming amidst the flock. Jude realizes the problem as now already present.

3. Jude warns of the serious consequences of unbelief. He uses the Old Testament examples of Israel's unbelief (5), the unbelief of the fallen angels, which manifested itself in rebellion (6), and that of Sodom and Gomorrah (7). This is climaxed with Jude's future reference as to what he will do to "ungodly" sinners (14-15). Here the key word is *remembrance*.

4. In this epistle there is a careful correlation drawn between correctness of doctrine and holy living. Jude emphasizes this by admonitions against ungodliness. Three examples are taken from the Old Testament of ungodliness. Cain as a picture of willful sin, Balaam as a picture of the sin of greed, and Korah as a picture of being presumptuous (11). By these examples, Jude also characterizes the false teachers of whom he warns. Here the key word is *woe*.

5. The closing verses (20-25) describe the responsibility of the believer in the face of increasing apostasy and ungodliness. In this section the key word is *keep*. Believers bear two responsibilities in the spiritual realm to himself. He is to build Himself up in the faith (20), pray in the Holy Spirit (20), and keep himself in the love of God. The second responsibility is to others: to have mercy on others (22-23), as he has received mercy from God (21); and to save some of them out of the fire (23).

Outline
I. Faith's Defense against Unbelief (1-4)
II. Faith's Departure into Unbelief (5-16)
III. Faith's Declaration Concerning Unbelief (17-25)

THIRTY

REVELATION

Introduction

The Book of Revelation was written by the Apostle John during the time that he was exiled on the isle of Patmos. It is a vision or revelation of Jesus Christ Himself given to the apostle, which deals with future events, with a strong word to the church and the ages that they represent.

The suggested overall theme for the Book of Revelation is that of the moral and spiritual conflict of the ages. The central figure of course is the Lamb of God, who is the final victor over all the allied powers of evil.

There have been copious books and theories written regarding this book. We will not take time to try to review all the various theories in regards to the Book of Revelation. There are more books then enough written on this topic. It is clearly a revelation of the goodness, grace, and mercy of God culminated in the coming of the Lamb and the great triumph in which all who believe in Christ shall enjoy. Whatever our beliefs, any teaching on the Book of Revelation should lead us to a deeper relationship with the Lord, and hope in Christ triumphant. Our Lord Come!

Heaven

1. This Revelation was directed towards the seven churches of Asia Minor (1:11). Persecution from without and serious problems within were

threatening the churches. The date of the writing may be placed about 90-95 AD.

2. The Book of Revelation is apocalyptic. The term means "to reveal" or "to uncover" something which has been veiled beforehand. Characteristic of apocalyptic Scripture, the book is written in signs and symbols. John states that the message was "sent and signified" (1:1). There are between three and four hundred symbols in the Book of Revelation. The secret to understanding the symbols of the book is to trace the symbols back to their Old Testament origins and to understand their usage there. Scripture interprets itself.

3. There are four main schools of interpretation of the book. The Preterist view understands the greater part of the book as fulfilled in early church history. The Historical view understands the entire book as being fulfilled during the present age. The Futurist view understands the greater part of the book as pertaining to events in the end time. The Idealist view understands the book as symbolic of the conflict between good and evil, with no reference to specific time.

4. The numerology of the book is elaborate and strikingly significant. The number four occurs frequently: four living creatures before the throne; four angels at the four corners of the earth, holding the four winds, etc. The number seven is even more prominent; seven Churches, seven candlesticks, seven stars, seven seals, seven trumpets, seven vials, seven thunders, seven spirits, the Lamb with seven horns and seven eyes, the seven-headed beast, seven mountains, and seven kings.

5. The Revelation speaks of the reality of the world to come. The present world has its sorrows, evils, and heartaches, but these things cannot enter the world to come. Revelation presents heaven not as a place of escape, but as a place of fellowship for those who have been faithful to the Lamb of God.

6. Whereas the teachings about the end are in terms of blessing with God for the redeemed, separation and punishment away from God is decreed for the unrighteous. Judgment moves throughout the book. Judgments meted out in seven-fold issues (seven seals, seven Trumpets, seven vials, etc.) are detailed in the book. This is the climactic culmination of the fulfillment of the promised Day of the Lord. Not only the final judgments on earth are described but the final judgments of the righteous and unrighteous unto eternal life or damnation (20:5-11).

Outline (The outline of the book is given in 1:19)
I. Write the Things Which Thou Hast Seen (1:1-20)
II. Write the Things Which Are (2:1-3:21)
III. Write the Things Which Shall Be Hereafter (4:1-22:5)

Printed in the United States
21747LVS00002B/376-423